I Was a Police Officer

Amite City and Baton Rouge City Police Departments

The Beginning of a Forty-Six-Year Career

By

Donald R. Smith

Copyright © 2025 Donald R. Smith

Preface

"I Was a Police Officer" reflects my experiences as a police officer in both Amite City and Baton Rouge. In my previous book, *I Never Saw It Coming*, I outlined my forty-six-year career in law enforcement, detailing my time with the Amite City and Baton Rouge police departments, as well as my roles in federal law enforcement.

This book will pick up where *I Never Saw It Coming* left off. I will describe my work as a police officer before transitioning into federal government service. I will discuss my experiences in uniform patrol, as a detective, a narcotics agent, in homicide, and in the motorcycle division.

I aim to write about each position I have held, exploring the details of every role, including the benefits and drawbacks of working in them. Please note that the information in this book is based on my memories and the daily journals I kept during that time. It is a combination of my opinions and personal experiences that allows me to write this book.

I also plan to write additional books focusing on my time in federal law enforcement. These will outline the various positions I held, describe job responsibilities, and include sample cases. So, keep an eye out for what's coming.

Acknowledgement

I would like to sincerely thank Chief J. C. Ricks of Amite, Louisiana. Without the opportunity he provided to join the Amite Police Department (APD), I can't imagine what I would be doing now. His trust enabled me to pursue a dream that led to a 46-year career.

I would also like to thank the officers I collaborated with at the APD who took the time to share their knowledge. They weren't required to, but they chose to engage with me and explain their approach to policing.

I would like to thank all the officers, detectives, and narcotics agents I worked with at the Baton Rouge City Police (BRPD). Several became like brothers, and we always looked out for each other, willing to do anything to protect one another. Even now, I try to stay in touch with some, but as we get older, everyone tends to focus on their families. It's as if we've moved on from that old life, and sometimes we try to forget those days.

I sincerely thank Almighty God for granting me the strength, knowledge, and opportunity to build a career in law enforcement. Without His guidance and mercy, I wouldn't have faced the daily challenges of my long career. Over 46 years of service, I have been shot at, stabbed, beaten, and left for dead multiple times, but I remain standing. As I age, healing becomes more difficult, but I keep going. Ha!

Finally, I want to thank everyone who has supported me in completing this book and my future endeavors. My wife, Linda, has been a constant source of encouragement for my writing. Keep in mind that much of what I put into these books, Linda has never seen before. When she proofreads some of my work, it is the first time she encounters it. I don't think I could love a woman more than I love Linda.

My son Jacob, the feeling I get when he says, "I'm proud of you, Dad," is unexplainable.

Table of Contents

Preface i

Acknowledgement ii

Introduction 1

Chapter 1 3

Getting My Start 3

Chapter 2 6

Auxiliary Police Officer 6

Chapter 3 13

Amite Police Officer 13

    House for Sale 18

    The Possum Incident 20

    APD Motorcycle Unit 23

    B. Stern & Company 25

    Salt and Pepper 26

    Officer Jeff Austin 30

    Amite Police Training 39

    Working Two Jobs 41

    Hope with BRPD 42

Chapter 4 44

Saying Goodbye to APD 44

Chapter 5 46

Baton Rouge Police 46

First Official Orders 48

Special Police Operations Team (SPOT) 54
Working Concerts 57
Special Assignment to Narcotics 62
Not All Goes Right 69
Surveillance on Victims 76
Store Watch 81
Stabbed in the Right Knee 87
Commendations 89
Permanent Transfer to Narcotics 90
Marijuana "Trees" 91
Wellness Check 95
Chapter 6 98
Working Undercover 98
Preparing for Undercover Work 100
Getting Attached 107
Chapter 7: Take a Step Back 112
Motorcycle Division 112
Back to Uniform Patrol 118
Chapter 8: Small Town Police vs. Large City Police . 120
Chapter 9: Dealing with Stress 124
Chapter 10: Ethics and Integrity 127
Conclusion 130
Federal Law Enforcement 134

Introduction

Before working as a Special Agent with the Department of Homeland Security, I was a police officer. My primary responsibility was to serve and protect lives and property. This included defending people from deception, maintaining peace, and upholding the constitutional rights of everyone.

I led a clean life and tried to set a good example for others. I did my best to remain calm and display courage when confronted with danger. I practiced complete self-control, always considering the well-being of others. I kept confidential information private, only disclosing it when necessary to fulfill my professional duties.

I never allowed personal feelings, biases, resentments, or friendships to influence my law enforcement decisions. I relentlessly pursued the prosecution of wrongdoers and enforced the law without fear, favoritism, malice, or ill will. I refrained from using unnecessary force or violence and never accepted gratuities.

My badge symbolized trust and my dedication to upholding the ethical standards of law enforcement. I continually prioritized these values, committing myself to both God and my career.

I was a sincere, dedicated, and reliable police officer. My integrity held greater significance to me than anything else in law enforcement.

Chapter 1

Getting My Start

As discussed in my first book, I Never Saw It Coming, after graduating from high school, I began working in August 1975 at Avondale Shipyard in New Orleans. I needed the job because Linda and I were getting married in September, and I knew we couldn't get married without a steady income.

Our wedding took place on September 12, 1975, and we rented an apartment in Amite to live in.

It was on a rainy day in May 1976 when I was off work at Avondale due to the weather. I sat in our apartment and decided to act on something I had been thinking about for a long time. I had always wondered what it would be like to be a police officer. I recall watching police vehicles drive around town and imagining what it would be like to work in that profession. I suppose you could call it an internal calling, because I felt drawn to that type of work, yet I kept those thoughts to myself.

I was concerned about the salary of a police officer in Amite and knew it wouldn't be much, but I was willing to give it a chance and try to make it work.

Why did I want to be in law enforcement or become a police officer? I gave it considerable thought. To my knowledge, no one in my family had ever worked in law enforcement, and I had never personally known anyone in the field. So how did I become involved in this profession? What pushed me toward it? I don't have a definitive answer to those questions. Even today, I recognize that I tried it, enjoyed doing it, and committed myself to it. Once I started, I never thought about leaving—until forty-six years later.

I often contemplate why others pursue careers in law enforcement. Is it because they have a family member in the field, creating a sense of obligation to follow in their footsteps? Or perhaps they're like me—the first in their family to embrace the idea independently. It certainly isn't for the wealth, as one doesn't become rich as a police officer, at least not in the conventional sense. Regardless of an individual's reasons for entering the profession, it is commonly said that a significant motivation is the desire to help or serve the community in some way.

I've heard that some individuals are inspired by action movies where police officers are portrayed as heroes—though, at times, they're also depicted as corrupt or self-serving. Still, many dream of becoming police officers in the hope of embodying heroism.

Anyway, back to that morning: I went to Amite City Hall and submitted my application to become a member of the police department. It didn't take long to complete the application, and when I finished, I drove back home. Honestly, I thought I would never hear anything more about it—but at least I could say I tried.

As I headed home, I reflected deeply on the direction of my life. I wasn't content with the daily commute from Amite to New Orleans. Still, the idea of becoming a police officer captivated me enough to take that first step and submit the application.

Chapter 2

Auxiliary Police Officer

Shortly after returning home from filing my application, I heard a knock at the front door. When I answered, a police officer standing there introduced himself as Chief J.C. Ricks. He said he had reviewed my application and was curious about my interest in joining the Amite Police Department. I told him I was highly interested, and we settled on the front porch to discuss the possibility of working for the department.

After a great discussion about the job functions and requirements, Chief Ricks recommended that I begin as an auxiliary officer. This role would allow me to work on weekends and explore whether law enforcement was truly the right path for me—before committing to a full-time position and the training that would come with it. When Chief Ricks made the suggestion, I saw it as my chance to eventually secure a full-time spot on the force.

After speaking with Chief Ricks, I felt like I had gained a foothold and progressed further than I could have imagined that day. A passing thought had led to an application, and that same day, the Chief himself showed up at my door.

I began riding along with other officers, learning as much as possible about all aspects of law enforcement—at least everything the Amite Police Department had to offer. I was nineteen years old at the time and primarily worked on weekends, covering parades, festivals, and special events while still employed at Avondale Shipyard.

I genuinely wanted to pursue this work as a career. I had started at Avondale because I needed a job to support Linda and me as we got married, but now, I had my foot in the door for what could become my life's work.

One thing was for sure: the salary at APD would not compare to what I made at Avondale. Still, I was willing to accept that because I wanted to gain experience in law enforcement and determine if this was truly the right path for me. By that point, I had already made up my mind: if I were offered a full-time position, I would take it. The salary? We would find a way to make it work.

The city of Amite is a small town in Tangipahoa Parish, with approximately 4,000 residents within its city limits. During my time there, the Amite Police Department consisted of a Chief of Police, an Assistant Chief, a Captain, and around six to eight officers at any given time. The department provided 24/7 protection for the city's residents and businesses, with officers patrolling the streets to ensure public safety.

I fully committed myself to the auxiliary officer program and worked diligently to learn as much as I could, with the goal of securing a full-time position. Chief Ricks provided me with essential job tools, including a badge, credentials, a uniform, a gun belt, and accessories. However, APD did not issue a service weapon, so I had to purchase one myself. I bought a Smith & Wesson Model 19—a six-shot .357 Caliber revolver—from Thompson's Sporting Goods in downtown Amite.

Linda was kind enough to give me a small, high-back wooden chair to place next to our bed. When I wasn't working, I would hang my gun belt and uniform on that chair. I also kept all my police-related items on it—paperwork, traffic violation codes, criminal codes I was studying, and other important materials. I was fully committed, studying constantly and immersing myself completely in the job.

Each morning, as I headed off to Avondale, I'd glance at that chair and see it as a symbol of opportunity. It represented my future. I took pride in everything it held.

When I worked weekends, I usually stayed out most of the night—or at least until the town quieted down. The experience varied depending on the officer I was riding with. Some of the older officers preferred not to get involved unless absolutely necessary. On the other hand, some of the younger officers enjoyed engaging in all kinds of situations. I was the same way—I wanted to be involved so I could learn. The more I experienced, the more knowledge I gained. I aimed to understand how each situation was handled.

I recall my first day as an auxiliary. I anticipated seeing officers at different levels of uniform readiness, understanding that it wouldn't be me. Indeed, some senior police officers arrived in wrinkled uniforms with unpolished boots. However, that didn't mean I could show up for my shift like that. I understood that my reputation began on day one!

The senior officers I was assessing had already established their reputations. I felt it was expected of me to arrive at each shift in a neat uniform with polished shoes. I received some sarcastic comments about how crisp my uniform was and how shiny my boots looked, but I recognized this as just part of the process. Overall, I believed my attire was suitable.

As a rookie, my peers considered my effectiveness useless. However, I was determined to change that perception by adding value during patrols. This involved taking the lead on calls and volunteering to stay late when needed. I understood that gaining experience was crucial for my growth, as I wanted to become an asset and quickly adapt to my new profession.

I realized that every officer had their own style of managing incidents. I observed each one and used those observations to begin shaping my own approach. I questioned whether I should jump right into situations or take time to assess things. Ultimately, I decided I would always strive to treat others the way I wanted to be treated.

As an auxiliary officer, I performed routine law enforcement duties alongside full-time officers who supported and guided me. I provided traffic and crowd control during parades, festivals, and other community events, helping to maintain peace and order. I also participated in foot and vehicle patrols.

Occasionally, the Chief would ask us to walk the main streets late at night and check business doors to ensure they were secure. We'd leave a tag on each door indicating it had been checked at a specific time. I also assisted with backup during traffic stops, crime scenes, and DWI checkpoints. I genuinely enjoyed feeling like I was contributing to the safety of my community.

I learned a great deal during this time. For example, deciding whether to issue a traffic citation during a stop was always left to the officer's discretion. If the violator was cooperative and admitted the mistake, I could issue a warning, a standard citation, or no citation at all. That kind of judgment call is a serious responsibility—especially for a young officer just starting out. I can understand how some young officers might let that power go to their heads or misuse it.

In all my interactions, I made every effort to be fair. In a small town, it doesn't take long to realize that your friends, neighbors, and local business owners are the same people you encounter on duty. I must have heard it a thousand times—"the people pay your salary." That reality shaped how I approached my responsibilities.

After working in the role for several months, people in the community who didn't know me before started recognizing me. There were residents who genuinely cared about the police department, and they got to know the officers. While some went out of their way to be friendly, others simply didn't like the police. That came with the territory.

I quickly learned to accept criticism as a chance to grow. I understood the importance of staying professional and respectful, even when faced with negative opinions. I learned to navigate difficult situations, to listen carefully, and to ask questions to fully understand the perspectives of others. I welcomed constructive feedback, which helped me de-escalate many situations.

As my confidence grew in the role of auxiliary officer, I began seriously considering a full-time career in law enforcement. That meant resigning from Avondale and accepting a smaller salary—but I was fully prepared to make that commitment.

Chapter 3

Amite Police Officer

In December 1976, Chief Ricks approached me and offered me a full-time position with the Amite Police Department (APD), marking the start of my extensive forty-six-year law enforcement career. Of course, I accepted, but I had to resign from my job at Avondale Shipyard and give them two weeks' notice. That was scary, too. I initially needed that job so Linda and I could get married, but later I acted on instinct and secured my position with the APD. Honestly, I was happy.

When I first began, our police station was a small cinderblock structure that lacked jail cells. It was positioned at the southeast corner of Hwy 51 and Hwy 16 in the downtown area, next to the railroad tracks. The primary police office was located behind the City Hall building. The APD operated from this small building for about eighteen years before moving to a new police station in the renovated train depot across the street.

The new station provided us with the space to perform our duties properly and to place someone in a city jail cell without needing to go to the Tangipahoa Parish Sheriff's Office for booking procedures. The new station included several rooms for processing suspects and conducting interviews and interrogations as needed. We also had a dedicated area for efficiently drafting and organizing traffic accident reports. With our dispatcher now located in the same building, we could obtain information more quickly and receive better assistance.

Working full-time, I learned a great deal and became more confident in my work. I could no longer rely too heavily on fellow officers, as I had to make decisions independently. Everyone viewed me as a regular officer and expected me to handle situations with minimal assistance. I needed to make decisions—right choices—and then stand by them. Sometimes, the decisions might not be correct, but if you learn from them, it becomes a learning experience.

The patrol vehicles were gray, equipped with blue bubble lights on top, identified as Unit #1 and assigned to Chief Ricks. Units #2 and #3 were manned by the officers on duty. Most of the time, I drove Unit #2, a comfortable Ford Crown Victoria. Police Unit #3 was a Chevrolet Impala, which rode well, but I always preferred the Ford for its greater comfort.

When I began patrolling alone, I feared that someone might stop me to ask a question I couldn't answer, which would make me appear unprofessional; however, that also motivated me to continue learning and reviewing scenarios in my head. I kept an Amite City map in my car to consult whenever the dispatcher called. I could check the address on the city map to locate my destination. However, it didn't take long before I learned all the streets and could respond without needing the map. Keep in mind that in the 1970s, we didn't have Waze, GPS, or cell phones to assist us.

While patrolling the city, I became increasingly comfortable and confident in my role. I responded promptly to police calls, managed motor vehicle accidents, and wrote police reports for various incidents. I suddenly felt like a regular police officer, making good, clear decisions with no issues.

Serving as a police officer involves patrolling the city, making traffic stops, writing reports, collecting evidence, arresting criminals, searching databases, responding to emergencies, and testifying in court. It required dedication, courage, and a commitment to upholding the law. The experience I gained will undoubtedly assist me in my next endeavor, whatever that may be.

As a full-time officer, I was responsible for completing various paperwork and administrative tasks. I have always been highly organized and developed strategies to ensure I completed my paperwork promptly. I was well-versed in multiple police databases, using them to store and retrieve information quickly and accurately.

I also understood the importance of confidentiality, so I took all necessary precautions when handling sensitive information. I took great pride in ensuring that all my paperwork was accurate and current, and I always double-checked my work before submitting it.

Maintaining both physical and mental fitness was crucial. I consistently prioritized getting at least eight hours of sleep each night and taking regular breaks. I followed a steady exercise regimen that kept me physically fit and energized. Furthermore, I aimed to stay healthy and alert during my duties.

Working in a small town with over 4,000 people can be challenging at times. Most often, your job involved ensuring security and that everything in the city ran smoothly. Occasionally, you might encounter an incident that required your response, or you might need to address a shoplifter at one of the stores during your shifts.

There were nights when people reported hearing noises outside their home windows while trying to sleep. I often responded to those calls, but it never turned out to be anything significant. I checked for footprints beneath the windows, sat outside, and listened for a while, but never found anything unusual. Still, you had to be the nice police officer there to serve and protect. You informed the complainant that you would patrol the area and monitor their home for the rest of the night. They thanked you for your efforts, and you wanted them to be satisfied because they were voters, and you needed the Chief to keep his job, so you were sure to keep yours.

Then there were the traffic violations. You see the violator; they are your friend or a contributor to the police department. So, do you go after them and pull them over? You can, but you have to do it in a friendly manner. The last thing you need is for everyone to get mad at you for stopping them. Besides, if you write them a ticket, they will go straight to the Chief and deliver it to him. You can rest assured that if it is near election time, the Chief will have to play the game and somehow take care of the ticket. The person then walked off with the attitude that they know someone and can get tickets resolved, and they look at you as if to say, "I told you so."

During my time at APD in the 1970s, writing tickets wasn't a requirement. Therefore, we didn't have to issue many tickets. We issued traffic citations, and most of them were paid. You must remember that the people you see on the streets are residents who live, work, and vote in the town. You balance effective law enforcement with compassion for the individuals you encounter. You can do nothing but accept it and understand that you are working in a small-town environment.

House for Sale

Due to the amount of time we spent together, whether working or off duty, the officers developed strong relationships and felt like a second family or a work family. As a law enforcement family, we found moments to relax and play pranks on each other, and the Chief was not excluded.

One day, Chief Ricks and his wife decided to build a new house in Amite. After completing it, the Chief chose to take a break and enjoy a short vacation. While they were away, all the officers monitored the house to ensure its security. One night during patrol, everything was quiet, and an auxiliary officer, Harold Henderson, rode with me.

As we patrolled around town, I noticed that Harold had brought a "For Sale" sign with him. I asked him what he planned to do with it, and he said he didn't know yet. Harold often requested that I drive by the Chief's house to check on it, but I had already visited several times and found everything in order. While we were patrolling, Harold quickly mentioned he had an idea: he wanted to put the sign in the front yard of the Chief's newly constructed home. We pulled up to the house, and I stopped so Harold could get out and place the sign in the yard. It read, "For Sale, Now."

It was funny, but no one was going to call the Chief about the house. Besides, I assumed Harold would pick up the sign before he went home. But he didn't. The next day, it wasn't long before the Chief began receiving phone calls inquiring about his new house for sale. He must have received numerous calls, as he returned from vacation to remove the sign from his yard. He also demanded to know who had placed the sign there, but no one revealed Harold's involvement.

The Chief blamed Captain Jerry Trabona, thinking he was responsible, but Jerry knew nothing about it. I knew that for a fact because I was present when Harold put it there. Jerry was unfairly bearing the brunt of the Chief's frustration, but actions like that couldn't stay secret for long in a small-town police department. All the officers discovered what had happened because Harold couldn't keep his mouth shut, but I never mentioned anything to anyone.

Of course, the Chief realized that someone from the department had placed the sign; however, he couldn't figure out who it was. He accused several other people until Harold finally stepped up and decided to tell the truth. Harold laughed it off, telling the Chief that at least now he knew people were interested in buying his house. I don't recall the Chief laughing about it too much, but he took the joke in good spirit. Poor Jerry took the brunt of the heat, but he eventually laughed it off as well. It's funny; the Chief never accused me!

The Possum Incident

Some days at work are busier than others, but there are also days when nothing seems to happen. You might work an entire shift with only one or two response calls. On slow days, when you aren't busy, you get creative and think of ways to pass the time, even if it means playing tricks on one another or someone else.

That said, I recall one night when I was on duty at 10:00 p.m. Four or five of us gathered outside the old police station, talking. We were changing shifts and couldn't fit inside the old station, so we stood outside and discussed the day's activities. Nothing much was happening, and it seemed like it would be a quiet night.

There was a group of individuals known as the Tangipahoa Parish Sheriff's Office CB Auxiliary Deputies, but I never fully understood their responsibilities. They patrolled at night and reported any unusual activity to the Tangipahoa Parish

Sheriff's Office radio dispatcher, all of which was conducted via their CB radios. However, they never became involved in any law enforcement activities, as they were essentially the eyes and ears on the roadways for deputies.

I recall that each one had a CB radio in their vehicle and an antenna extending high into the air. It was as if they had their own club and would sometimes meet in town to talk on a corner somewhere. I remember stopping and speaking with them one night, and they congratulated one of their peers for coming forward after observing a traffic accident and reporting it to the Tangipahoa Sheriff's Office. That was the kind of work they performed, and they took it very seriously.

This young man from Roseland, who was in his early twenties, actively participated in that CB auxiliary group. He would often come by the old police station, especially if he saw us all standing around talking outside. I don't remember his name, but they called him "Red Horse." He drove a small car that looked like it would fall apart at any minute. He had a tall CB antenna on the back of his vehicle that protruded into the air, and as he drove around, the antenna would lie back due to the wind.

On that particular night, he pulled up to the old station where we were all gathered and exited his vehicle. As he walked around among us, not saying much, the Chief and someone else had just caught a possum behind the old station. The Chief put the possum in a brown burlap sack; I don't know why and never asked. Sometimes, the less you know, the better off you are.

When Red Horse exited his vehicle, he began walking around without paying attention to his surroundings. The Chief took the sack with the possum and, while Red Horse wasn't looking, dumped it onto the back floorboard of Red Horse's car.

Not long after, Red Horse got back into his vehicle and started driving away on Highway 51 from the police station, headed back toward Roseland. The poor guy didn't get too far before the car swerved all over the roadway and eventually came to a stop. Red Horse jumped out of his vehicle, not knowing what was running around in his car.

We all laughed so hard watching his reaction. Red Horse grabbed a paper bag and lit it on fire, attempting to smoke the possum out from under the front seat. Doing this ended up setting his interior driver's seat ablaze. The possum escaped, but the driver's seat was burned. Red Horse had to wait a bit for the springs in the seat to cool down before he could drive home.

He told us he was driving along when something started crawling on him. I can assure you that Red Horse was okay, and we sent him on his way home to Roseland. We laughed so hard and talked about that for a long time. I don't believe he ever found out who put the possum in his vehicle. But one thing was for sure: we did not see him for a long time.

Now, let me explain something. Yes, we played tricks, crazy schemes, and harassed one another on occasion, but we also took our jobs seriously and worked hard protecting the community. We worked and solved many criminal cases occurring around town. But also remember, this was Amite, and although you worked like a big city police department, well, this was Amite. Enough said!

APD Motorcycle Unit

Here is something not many people know about. Believe it or not, the Amite Police Department "almost" had a motorcycle unit. That is true! One officer on the force, Dave, wanted to become a motorcycle officer for the APD and had his motorcycle to donate to the cause. For some time, Dave rode to and from work on his motorcycle while in uniform, trying to convince the Chief and others that the department could benefit from a motorcycle unit. He often discussed using the motorcycle unit to address traffic issues and vehicle accidents while achieving lower patrol costs with gas.

I'm sure Dave had good intentions with his thoughts and plans, but in Amite? Come on! We never experienced any significant traffic problems; however, we occasionally had car accidents, and night patrols were vital. That was my thought, along with just about everyone else's, so how does a motorcycle fit into the APD?

Dave continued to advocate for riding a motorcycle for some time, with the Chief consistently denying the request. Consequently, Chief Ricks decided to put an end to this at the city council meeting, proposing the idea of having a motorcycle for department use. However, that suggestion didn't gain much traction with the council members. The issues surrounding insurance and the purchase of a motorcycle led the city council to dismiss the idea before it could take off.

I believe the Chief did this to show Dave that the idea wouldn't materialize. Furthermore, none of us grasped the concept, particularly at that time. A motorcycle, in Amite?

However, I wanted to let you know that the thought was once present, and that's how close the APD came to acquiring a motorcycle unit.

B. Stern & Company

B. Stern and Company was a large department store in Amite, situated at the northwest corner of Hwy 51 and Hwy 16. B. Stern closed its doors sometime in the 1980s, and a Shell service station currently occupies that corner.

B. Stern was a busy store that employed a night security guard named Coot Carrier. Coot had a slight disability that I believe resulted from a previous stroke. He was working for B. Stern when I joined the APD and had been there for years.

When I left the APD in 1979, Coot was still employed there. B. Stern was an all-around store offering various products, including hardware, clothing, shoes, and other items. During Christmas, an abundance of toys was displayed in the large window.

Coot came on duty around 10:00 p.m. each night and worked until 6:00 a.m. the following morning. I got to know him very well, and for some reason, he nicknamed me "Motor Oil," a name he used throughout our time together. I genuinely don't know where that nickname originated, but that's what he called me, and I accepted it.

Coot enjoyed listening to French Cajun music on his truck radio throughout the night. Each evening, he would park his truck outside the store, and as I passed by, I could hear the tunes from inside.

During the summer months, he would roll down the window, letting the music carry across the street to the station. He mentioned that while he didn't grasp all the lyrics, he still liked the music immensely.

During the Christmas season, B. Stern adorned the store windows with holiday decorations, showcasing toys for children to admire. Coot took me through the store after midnight to reveal the available items before anyone else. He made his rounds, and I sometimes joined him for company.

After leaving the APD and working for the federal government, I learned he had passed away. Coot was a man who took his job as a security guard seriously. To my knowledge, no one attempted to break in or damage the property while Coot was on duty.

Salt and Pepper

I made many friends in the Amite Police Department and worked with each officer on various occasions. I learned something from every officer; however, this does not mean I agreed with their techniques or incorporated their ideas into my work ethic.

I observed, listened, and learned from each officer, then adapted their behaviors to suit my own. Everything I was involved in emphasized ethics, honesty, and completing tasks, and I felt proud of my work and what I accomplished.

One officer I grew particularly fond of was Pete Richardson. An African American, Pete and I patrolled together whenever we could, mainly during the late-night shift from 10:00 p.m. to 6:00 a.m. Our extensive time together allowed us to handle numerous police incidents, earning us a reputation in the APD, Tangipahoa Sheriff's Office, and the community as "Salt and Pepper." Naturally, I was the salt, and Pete was the pepper.

Pete and I were responsive to everything happening around town, and we feared nothing because we had each other's backs. Pete taught me a great deal about police work, particularly in how to interact with the community. He knew everyone and guided me on whom to trust and whom to avoid. Soon, I discovered that some people are simply crazy.

When night fell and everything slowed down, Pete would take me into some of the town's tougher bars. Everyone in those bars knew Pete, and eventually, they got to know me well, too. They quickly discovered that Pete and I were good friends, and before long, I could enter any of those establishments on my own without any issues. It reached a point where I could resolve problems and disputes peacefully in those bars, and I owe all that to Pete.

When Pete and I began working together, he would take me into what we called the "tough" bars in town to introduce me to everyone.

On one occasion, late one night, Pete and I responded to a disturbance at one of the bars. Once we had settled everything, Pete called for everyone's attention. He introduced me and said, "For God's sake, nothing better happen to him in this bar." No one said anything after Pete spoke, and I can honestly say that no one ever gave me a tough time in those bars. I soon became good friends with many people in the Black community.

Pete liked me from the moment we first met. He took me under his wing, teaching and protecting me. Pete was one of the officers who motivated me to work hard and excel. I always looked forward to working with him each night, knowing it would be a valuable learning experience.

Pete was a remarkable man and an exceptional friend who taught me about being a police officer and interacting with people.

Pete and I had fun working together, and we also enjoyed our late-night moments when everything was "dead." Pete's family owned a funeral home in Amite, across from Amite High School.

On numerous occasions, Pete and I discussed how autopsies are performed and how bodies are prepared for funerals. Pete knew I wanted to learn everything about police work and aspired to join a larger police agency someday, so I needed to understand all aspects of death cases.

I learned a great deal about death and how funeral homes prepare bodies for viewings at funerals. This may sound strange now, but at that time, I was learning what I believed was part of police work and absorbing everything I could.

As I noted, Pete was aware of my interest in potentially moving to the Baton Rouge Police Department (BRPD). He made efforts to prepare me for the challenges I might face ahead. Pete also understood that working with other agencies would expose me to death and require me to observe autopsies related to law enforcement cases, so he wanted to ensure I was familiar with this process.

Unfortunately, years after I left the APD and began working for the federal government, I learned that Pete was killed in an automobile accident. I was informed that he had suffered a heart attack while driving and veered off the road, hitting a tree.

Officer Jeff Austin

Officer Jeff Austin played a pivotal role in inspiring my perspective on law enforcement. He was an older gentleman who had previously served with the BRPD before he joined the Amite Police Department. While I am unsure of the exact duration of Jeff's tenure with the APD prior to my arrival, I do know that it was several years.

We all enjoyed playing around with Jeff; everyone teased him at work. However, Jeff was the type of guy who kept to himself and never got involved in anyone else's business. He always worked the late shift, finishing his duties at 6:00 a.m. each morning. Jeff told me he slept better during the day than at night.

Jeff worked hard to hide his smoking from his family, so everyone teased him about confessing to his wife, which made him anxious as he extinguished his cigarette.

I recall working with Jeff in the early morning hours, sitting at the police station while we waited for the next shift to start at 6:00 a.m. The Chief or someone else would walk in while Jeff was smoking in the station, and the first thing they would say was, "Jeff, your wife is here to pick you up from work."

Jeff would jump up, scrambling to put out his cigarette and trying to get the smell off his clothes, but it didn't take long before he realized it was just a joke. He would then storm out of the station to start his walk home.

Jeff walked home from the police station almost every morning along Old Hwy 51, about half a mile south of the station. He always claimed he walked for exercise, but I suspected he used that time to smoke in peace. It was amusing that Jeff smoked a lot, constantly burning tiny holes in his police shirt and always having ashes on him. He was perpetually cleaning himself up, so I don't think Jeff was hiding his smoking as well as he thought.

Jeff took the ribbing from everyone in stride, and he never got mad because everyone cared about him. He had a big heart and extensive experience in police work. To this day, I still don't understand why he was never utilized more in training officers. Was it because Jeff was a loner and never engaged in anything that didn't pertain to him, or perhaps he didn't want to take on any training? I never knew.

While working night shifts, Jeff and I rode around town together, typically from 2:00 a.m. to about 3:30 a.m. During our rides, he shared stories from his time at BRPD. Some of the stories he told intrigued me and made me contemplate the possibility of working for BRPD someday. Jeff never volunteered information, but if I wanted to know something, I had to ask, and he would respond. When I inquired about police work, he provided incredibly detailed explanations and was very descriptive in his efforts to help me understand.

I often found Jeff somewhere to discuss his time working for the BRPD. I also remember thinking it would be nice if the stories he told me took place in Amite; however, Amite did not have the same rates of burglaries, thefts, car burglaries, fights, or murders as Baton Rouge.

Jeff shared insights about his training and duties at the BRPD, detailing how the work shifts functioned. He frequently talked about the BRPD, and I expressed my interest in joining over time. While Jeff was always open to my thoughts, he neither pushed me toward the idea nor discouraged me from it. He emphasized that the choice to work at BRPD was ultimately mine and advised me not to let others sway my decision.

As I mentioned, Jeff provided a detailed explanation of the BRPD and his work experience. He discussed patrolling the town with the driver's window rolled down. When we rode together and I was driving, it was cold outside, yet he would ask me to roll down the driver's window. I inquired why the window had to be down, and he explained that one would not hear anything while riding around the neighborhood with the driver's window rolled up. When he drove, he would cruise around town slowly with his driver's window down, listening out the window.

Jeff told me many stories about riding slowly with the driver's window rolled down so he could hear any glass breaking near a house or anyone screaming for help. He mentioned that on one occasion, while with the BRPD, he was driving through a community when he heard glass breaking near a home, so he pulled over and apprehended a suspect attempting to break into a house. From then on, I rode with my driver's window down, listening for anything unusual because it made sense. He also said that when all is calm late at night, one should turn off their vehicle's lights and drive slowly around town without lights, with the window down, and listen.

In my opinion, Jeff was a walking textbook of law enforcement information, and I absorbed all I could from him. To this day, I don't believe the other officers truly understood the wealth of information Jeff carried within him, but I did. I always felt that Jeff should have been more accustomed to teaching other officers about police work, just as he taught me.

Eventually, I spoke with Chief Ricks about my desire to

explore the possibility of working for the BRPD. Although I anticipated laughter, the Chief encouraged me to pursue it if that was my wish.

He assured me that he would not try to hold me back and motivated me to follow my ambitions-unique ambitions. I recall him mentioning that he understood I likely wouldn't stay for long and that I would seek other opportunities.

I recall discussing my goals with everyone in the department, and much to my surprise, they were all supportive, though with expressions of sadness about my departure. Honestly, there was a moment when I almost reconsidered staying with APD, believing I had a good job and felt comfortable there.

Chief Ricks gave me my start in law enforcement. Who knows what I might be doing now if he hadn't believed in me? Pete introduced me to the fundamentals of law enforcement and interpersonal skills. Jeff inspired me to consider a career with the BRPD and was pivotal in motivating my pursuit of this path. The influence of these three men has profoundly shaped my future, and I will always be grateful to them.

Working with APD was more than just pulling pranks on one another. We tackled solving crimes around town, such as burglaries, various thefts, and drug arrests. Being in a small town, there was always something to investigate.

I recall lawnmowers being stolen, cars being broken into, and numerous other types of crimes. We managed these incidents, made arrests, resolved cases, and returned property to its owners.

First Homicide Investigation

I want to share a story from my early days on the job, shortly after returning from a six-week law enforcement training at Louisiana State University. I need to be careful not to disclose any names or details that could embarrass anyone. I believe this story is important because it illustrates how quickly situations can develop, and it emphasizes the need for officers to react swiftly, take control, and act correctly.

It was a Sunday morning, and I was working the morning shift from 6 a.m. to 2 p.m. alone. Many Sundays, only one officer was assigned to work the morning shift until 2 p.m., when two more officers came on duty.

That morning, I was driving around town checking behind businesses to make sure nothing had been broken into overnight. I was then contacted by Amite Police dispatch, asking me to respond to a house to investigate a loud noise or possible gunshot.

I immediately drove to the house, and upon arrival, I noticed several people standing outside. I exited my vehicle and walked onto the porch. The people standing around began shouting for me to get in the house because there was a gunshot. I immediately stopped to observe the location and my surroundings, trying to catch a glimpse of what was inside the house. The front door was open, and I could see someone lying on the bed, shirtless. I stepped inside, and then I noticed a female standing on the left side of the bed.

On the bed was a white male, and I could observe a bullet hole in his chest. Lying next to the man was a six-shot revolver.

I approached the man, and the woman calmly stated she had shot him. I checked her over and, for security reasons, made sure she had no weapons before asking her to sit in a chair beside the bed. I then went to the man and used a small pillow to shift the weapon aside so I could examine him. I saw that he was still breathing, and based on the size of the bullet hole in his chest, it appeared to be from a large-caliber weapon.

While securing the area, dispatch contacted me via my portable radio to inform me that an ambulance was en route. I later found out that someone at the scene had called the police station, reporting that a man had been shot.

I observed the wound on the man, and at that moment it

was not bleeding. While I was waiting for the ambulance, I took a moment to look around the room and commit to memory the location of everything. The white female sat in the chair and was not saying much, other than that she had shot him. I didn't ask her any questions because I knew detectives from the sheriff's office would be conducting the investigation.

My main goal was to provide as much first aid as possible to the man, but I also had to keep an eye on the woman and remain aware of everything happening around me, all while trying to form a mental picture of how the scene looked when I arrived.

A few minutes later, the ambulance arrived, and they brought the stretcher into the bedroom. One of the ambulance drivers asked what had happened, and the woman said, "She shot him."

The ambulance transported the man to the nearby hospital, where he died shortly after arrival. The woman was taken into custody and charged accordingly by detectives from the Tangipahoa Sheriff's Office.

The point of me telling this story is simple. Here I am working on a quiet Sunday morning. All is calm, and I am thinking about what I need to do when I get off work. Then comes a call to check out a loud noise, possibly a gunshot.

Keep in mind that I have never worked a call like this in my short police career. I have been on the job for about six months and thought I was doing well.

This was the first time I walked in on a victim who had just been shot. I was also dealing with the suspect, keeping my eye on her, and trying to secure the scene all at the same time. All of this was happening on a Sunday morning!

At this point, my mind is racing at over 100 mph, trying to recall some training I recently received on collecting evidence. Was everything I'm doing right?

After the ambulance left the scene with the victim, I needed to gather all the names of everyone outside and get a quick statement from them. As I began, the Sheriff's Office arrived and started helping me. Man, what a relief.

After the Sheriff's Office arrived, I went to the hospital to see the victim, but he was already deceased.

I later met with Chief J.C. Ricks and gave him a rundown of everything that had taken place. We also met with the detectives from the Sheriff's Office and shared notes.

As a police officer, you never know what to expect on any given day. Luckily, I had recently received some fresh police training that helped me through the situation. I can also assure you that there were a few things I could have done better while at the scene, but overall, I was commended for my actions.

The female was charged and pleaded guilty to the shooting.

Police work is dangerous, some would argue more so now than before, and it is stressful and can be thankless. Yet, it is a vital cog in the machine that is society, and your decision to serve your community is both honourable and respected. However, that fact alone won't ensure your success in your new role as the face of public service.

I was among those who aimed to be proactive, ensuring I was present where I needed to be at the right time. My reputation served as my most crucial asset in law enforcement, capable of opening or closing opportunities throughout my career.

In law enforcement, a widely shared saying is: "Your reputation begins day one."

Amite Police Training

During my time with the APD, I underwent training that comprised the Police Officers Standard of Training (POST), a six-week law enforcement training course offered at LSU. Completing this training was necessary to qualify for state supplemental pay.

On August 8, 1977, I completed the Tangipahoa Parish Sheriff's Office (TPSO) Basic Law Enforcement Training course at the Tangipahoa Courthouse. Officers from various cities throughout the parish attended, and we received training in essential law enforcement techniques, laws, firearms, and defensive tactics.

On May 15, 1978, I received training and was certified to use the Doppler Radar Unit, also known as a radar gun. The radar was utilized to monitor speeding violators in town, particularly in school zones.

In September 1978, I participated in a six-week training program at the Louisiana State University (LSU) Law Enforcement Basic Training Academy. The curriculum included fundamental law enforcement courses, state law education, firearms skills, and self-defense strategies.

While working with the APD, I was commissioned by the TPSO in January 1977. This commission allowed me to assist the TPSO outside the Amite city limits as needed. If a TPSO deputy required help with a traffic stop or search warrant beyond the city limits, we had the authority to respond and assist. I maintained my commission until I left the APD and joined the BRPD.

As a new officer with APD, I spent a considerable amount of time working patrol on the night shift with the same officer, day in and day out. My partner and I had it down to a science; we knew each other so well that we could anticipate each other's every move.

I became close with several officers at APD, while others were simply colleagues with whom I got along well. I saw eye-to-eye with some officers and learned greatly from observing their performance. However, there were several whose tactics and handling of situations I didn't appreciate. This allowed me to observe everyone and how they conducted themselves, enabling me to develop my approach to doing what I felt was right. For the most part, though, I got along well with everyone, and we all seemed to help each other when needed.

Working Two Jobs

Earlier, I mentioned that the money working for the APD wasn't as good as what I was making with Avondale Shipyard. Well, it wasn't as good, but it wasn't too bad either. There were times when I worked two jobs to help make ends meet financially.

I once worked for Clemons Sawmill during the morning hours and then went to work for the APD on the night shift. I would get off work from APD each morning at 6:00 a.m., take a small nap, and be at Clemons for 7:00 a.m. I usually got off at 3:00 p.m. and returned home to eat and sleep a few hours before going back to the APD for 10:00 p.m.

I eventually left Clemons and went to work for Kent's Welding, working the same hours. But I did what I had to do to make ends meet. I could have stayed at Avondale or found another better-paying job somewhere, but I wanted to be a police officer. If it took two jobs for me to do it, then so be it.

Linda even pitched in and worked at several places so I could continue with the APD. She worked at the TG&Y for a short while and then went to work for the Royal Oak in Amite.

I felt compelled to trust my instincts and continue as a police officer. It became clear to me that this choice was correct, and I can genuinely affirm that it was the right one.

The sacrifices that Linda and I made for me to remain in law enforcement were worthwhile.

Hope with BRPD

After applying on April 16, 1979, I took the Baton Rouge Police Civil Service Test and passed. I received a letter from the Civil Service Board on May 4, 1979, stating that I was being considered for employment. I then underwent the interview process and a psychological evaluation.

I hoped the BRPD would be a place where I could continue my search for knowledge, build upon it, and discover even more. I genuinely wanted to do more, and I knew that working with the BRPD would increase my responsibilities for maintaining public safety, enforcing laws, and protecting a larger community. I understood that the officers at BRPD also played a crucial role in preventing and responding to various situations of criminal activity, ensuring the well-being of individuals and their property.

My decision to work for BRPD was influenced by my potential for longevity. I recognized opportunities for growth, advancement, and promotion, as well as the potential for special assignments. I sought an environment that utilized my skills and abilities, and I wanted to feel valued and have a sense of belonging.

I anticipated that the BRPD would assign me various responsibilities, including patrolling designated areas, responding to emergency calls, conducting investigations, making arrests, and issuing citations or warnings for infractions of the law. After speaking with many people and conducting research, I applied for the BRPD.

Chapter 4

Saying Goodbye to APD

Well, I did it. I said my goodbyes to everyone at the APD and received well-wishes, good luck, and pats on the back. On my last day as an APD officer, I gathered my belongings and looked around the station. I remember thinking that I didn't want to burn any bridges in case I had to come back. So, I ensured I was on solid ground with everyone, including Chief Ricks—just in case I had to come crawling back.

Leaving the APD was not easy. It was difficult because I had made many friends and was beginning to feel that I was positively impacting my community. Transitioning from the APD to the BRPD was a step up for me, but I had to ensure my decision was based on sound reasoning and careful consideration.

I remember saying goodbye to everyone and feeling a profound sense of emptiness. I had many good memories there and knew I would never lose them. Those memories will stay with me and, hopefully, help shape my future. I recall using these experiences as a source of comfort and strength when I began the academy. Each person I said goodbye to became a personal story, reminding me of my connection with them.

Every colleague I worked with created memories that showed how changes can lead to new beginnings. What would I have done if I had never met Jeff Alston and talked about the BRPD?

We can value the past while looking forward to the future, acknowledging that each ending carries the essence of new beginnings.

When we reflect on saying goodbye, it's essential to remember the beautiful moments associated with it. They enrich our lives and provide the courage to take the next step, knowing that we carry fragments of those experiences with us wherever we go.

I left the APD in June 1979, after two and a half years, to advance my career by attending the academy with the BRPD. As I mentioned earlier, Chief Ricks gave me my start in law enforcement, and I am incredibly grateful—because without him, I would not have enjoyed a long, forty-six-year career.

Everything came together through the Lord's blessings, and although I can't explain how, I knew I was on the path to a fulfilling law enforcement career.

Chapter 5

Baton Rouge Police

In June 1979, I began the twelve-week academy in Baton Rouge. The academy was comprehensive, encompassing basic law enforcement training in both criminal and civil law for city and state personnel, as well as extensive training in firearms, physical fitness, and self-defense.

When I started at the academy, I believed my prior police experience and confidence in my knowledge of police work would make it easy. However, I was hit with a harsh reality when I joined the BRPD academy, which turned out to be quite demanding. This experience unveiled aspects of police work I was previously unaware of.

The curriculum included classes on Louisiana state law, criminal and civil law, Baton Rouge City Codes, and vehicle violation regulations. Following these law classes, we explored the legal processes involved in evidence gathering for criminal cases, which included marking, identifying, and engaging in criminal procedure classes aimed at courtroom preparation.

The academy posed significant challenges, especially in physical training and firearms instruction. I recall developing blisters on my trigger finger from the extensive shooting sessions we conducted at the firing range.

Sometimes, I felt out of touch during the academy, just like many of my classmates. Because I had prior police experience, everyone looked to me for help and guidance. I didn't have the heart to tell them I didn't know any more than they did about many subjects.

During my law classes, I initially lacked experience and understanding of the training issues highlighted by the academy. However, the academy staff was exceptional and frequently offered us significant support, particularly after we reached the halfway point. Once we hit that milestone, every staff member was dedicated to ensuring that no one failed. If you had made it that far, you deserved to complete the program.

I remember Sergeant Robert Waymire, Lieutenant Anthony Martello, Corporal Ray Jackson, and Corporal Ronnie Borer, the essential staff members at the academy who provided us with tremendous support. Once we reached the halfway mark, they grew closer to us, showing a sincere desire for everyone to succeed and graduate.

Sgt. Waymire and I formed a strong friendship, chatting about all aspects of working for the BRPD. He had a deep love for the department and often fondly recalled the early days of his career. Sgt. Waymire provided tremendous support both during my time at the academy and afterward, and I leaned on him heavily, valuing his insights on various issues.

I graduated from the 40th Session of the BRPD Academy on August 29, 1979, at 2:00 p.m.

First Official Orders

On August 22, 1979, I received my initial official orders from the BRPD, directing me to report to the Uniform Patrol Division at Winbourne Station, located on Winbourne Avenue, on September 4, 1979, at 9:45 p.m. I was filled with excitement and empowerment, feeling like a genuine police officer ready to take on the city of Baton Rouge.

On September 4th, at 9:45 p.m., I reported for my first duty shift. I wore a brand-new uniform, ironed perfectly by Linda, and my badge was all too shiny. Upon my arrival at the station, I noticed officers walking into a large room with chairs and desks, so I followed them in. I sat down in the back of the room with my new uniform and shiny badge, waiting for roll call so I could say, "Here." I noticed officers looking at me, and I assumed they were just wondering who the new guy was.

Roll call started, and I waited patiently for my name to be

called, but it wasn't. Apparently, there was a mistake, and maybe they forgot to add my name. All the officers received assignments and were partnered together, and when roll call was over, everyone started leaving. Now, I was worried, so I walked up to the shift commander and introduced myself. He said, "Follow me." Great, now I was getting an assignment, too.

I followed him over to the wall where the schedules were posted. He looked around and found my name. Then, I heard those words: "You're off." What? He then showed me the schedule and said, "You're off tonight. Be back tomorrow at 9:45 p.m." Of course, the other officers standing there began doing what cops do best: laughing and making fun. I took it like a man; I didn't cry. I just laughed, shrugged my shoulders, and did what anyone else would do—walked out as fast as I could.

You can be assured that I quickly learned how to read a work schedule effectively, something I should have addressed sooner. Even though my start time for the night shift at Winbourne was set for that evening, I was scheduled off. I had previously received instructions to call and confirm my official work schedule, but I failed to follow through. This was the first lesson I picked up.

After feeling thoroughly embarrassed, I drove back home to Amite. During the drive, I felt discouraged because I had been eager to start my first shift, but now I had to wait until tomorrow night to return and try again. I also knew I would have to face it again tomorrow night at roll call.

Working in uniform patrol provided an outstanding foundation, allowing me to learn extensively from the officers in that role.

I aimed to understand every facet of police work. I partnered with various trainers, observing and learning extensively from them. The experience was thrilling; even as an APD officer, it was diminished in comparison to what I encountered with the BRPD.

I recall the first time I spoke on the police radio, fully aware that several hundred people were tuning in. The dispatcher, aware of my inexperience, would respond with, "Repeat, come again," each time I spoke. I'd raise my voice to repeat my message, only to hear her say, "Repeat, come again" once more. It seemed amusing to many as they started clicking their mics in response. I eventually understood that this was a tradition for welcoming new officers, as my training partner chuckled and explained. That was okay, but it didn't alleviate my embarrassment; I felt like a fool. Nonetheless, as the newcomer, I went along with it and accepted the situation, finding that it became easier over time.

Working in uniform patrol was a rewarding experience as we handled various police calls, from home burglaries and car thefts to disturbance reports and bar fights. I conducted traffic stops and issued tickets to violators, which helped me gain valuable experience interacting with various individuals and their behaviors. I quickly learned to settle down and adapt to the new work I was performing.

Eventually, I became more comfortable with the work and started to question the decisions made by the training officers. However, that was my second mistake.

After roll call one night, around 11:00 p.m., my training officer and I drove out toward Government Street and met up with two other patrol cars from the precinct. I knew who everyone was, and they started talking about the burglar and the type of vehicle he would be driving. They began discussing placing officers out for a stakeout to try to catch the bad guy. I was instructed to get out by the graveyard near Government Street and hide on the corner. If I saw the particular vehicle drive by, I would radio it in to the others so they could follow it. I got out with my portable radio, flashlight, and a light jacket because it was getting cool at night. I then started looking for a place to hide. My training officer told me to jump the fence into the graveyard and find a spot to hide.

Well, I did. I found a nice spot by a tree next to some gravestones. I waited, and waited, and waited. I never saw that car come by my location. I saw plenty of police units drive by, but not the bad guy. (It never occurred to me at the time why I was hiding out on a corner with police vehicles driving by.)

It's now 3:00 a.m., and I'm still in the graveyard, waiting. I convinced myself that this is what a stakeout entails, and if I want to pursue police work, this is part of the experience. Consequently, despite the freezing cold, I remained patient.

Finally, it's getting close to 5:00 a.m., and I'm now extremely cold, aggravated, and severely hungry. This was one of the longest nights I've ever spent. But hey, it was for a worthy cause—I was going to help catch a bad guy.

At 5:00 a.m., my training officer stopped in front of where I was located, instructing me to get in the vehicle. I hopped the fence and got in as instructed. I began giving him my report on what I hadn't seen during the night, but he didn't respond. We drove without speaking a word. I knew something wasn't right, and I started thinking, had I missed seeing the vehicle?

We arrived at an IHOP, where he dropped me off at the

front door before finding a parking spot. As I entered, I was greeted by the shift commander and several officers who were clapping for me. I was utterly taken aback by what was happening. When my training officer walked in, he warmly welcomed me to the force, mentioning that I had passed with flying colors. I wondered what I had done to earn this. They explained that, as a recruit, they were observing how long I would work without complaining or abandoning my assigned tasks. I succeeded in this because I worked all night without a word of complaint, doing what was asked of me. The shift commander noted that I lasted longer than many others. To celebrate, they all chipped in to buy me breakfast, and I enjoyed a hearty meal of steak and eggs along with two glasses of chocolate milk. That's right, two glasses of chocolate milk—because they were treating!

Fortunately, later on, I was able to play tricks on others as well, and it was more enjoyable to play the pranks than to be the one being pranked.

After months of training with officers, I patrolled solo in a police vehicle. At that moment, my confidence surged, and I felt I had made significant progress in my career. I was now a genuine police officer, mastering the intricacies of police work. I drove a patrol car independently with the BRPD.

As I mentioned earlier, I became friends with Sgt. Waymire, and we would discuss everything from working hard to building a good reputation and advancing through the ranks. He told me that, given my prior experience, I should learn things more quickly and easily advance up the ranks.

I once expressed my desire to become a detective and conduct criminal investigations, and he laughed, telling me to be patient and that it could happen in time. Sgt. Waymire said he liked me because I was a young man from a small police department striving to better myself in all aspects of life. I trusted him greatly and often called to speak with him whenever I had questions about the department.

Special Police Operations Team (SPOT)

I learned that the BRPD had the SPOT. Several years later, the name changed to "Street Crimes Unit." They were focused solely on investigating residential and vehicle burglaries and thefts. The detectives assigned to SPOT worked in plain clothes and were specially trained in home and vehicle burglary investigations. After making some inquiries, many officers informed me that one typically needs about five years of police experience before receiving consideration for assignment there.

In October 1979, I received a phone call from Sgt.

Waymire, who instructed me to write a letter to Sgt. E. Burns, the supervisor of SPOT, requesting an official transfer to that unit. He explained that an opening was forthcoming and believed it would be a suitable place for me to join as a detective, gaining more experience.

I wrote the transfer request letter and submitted it to Sgt. Burns for his consideration. Within a few days, he contacted me by phone to schedule an interview at the SPOT office. I remember being very excited, but I also knew that two other candidates were being interviewed and considered for the position.

On the day of my interview, I met Sgt. Burns, who turned out to be an extremely nice guy, and we talked for a long time. He asked me numerous questions about my experience working for the APD and my future aspirations. I answered his questions and felt that I had explained everything clearly.

After leaving the interview, I felt positive about it, but I also knew that the other two candidates had more police experience.

I learned later that one of the candidates was a good friend of Sgt. Burns. I accepted that whatever happened would happen; if it were meant to be, it would be. At the very least, I gained experience participating in the interview process.

Several days had passed since my interview, and I was now engaged in my work as a uniformed patrol officer, so I was not thinking about transferring. Unexpectedly, I received a phone call from Sgt. Burns, who welcomed me to the unit and said I should receive a transfer letter from the chief shortly.

After hanging up, I felt a mix of excitement and fear. It was a good feeling to know that Sgt. Burns trusted me and allowed me to come to SPOT with less than a year with the PD. I immediately called Sgt. Waymire at the academy to inform him, but he laughed at me because he had already been told. He said he was proud of me and wanted me to make the most of this situation.

I soon received a letter from the Chief stating that I had been reassigned to SPOT as a detective from the Uniform Patrol Division at Winbourne Station. That letter was the catalyst for everything. It was final—a done deal—I was going to SPOT to be a detective.

On November 1, 1979, I reported for my first day of duty at SPOT, where I was introduced to everyone, reviewed past cases, and learned the location of various office items. I was assigned to investigate residential burglaries and thefts, so I had to review case law and observe others at work. I was later partnered with a female detective who had more law enforcement experience than I did. Although I worked with other detectives in the unit, she became my permanent partner. We were assigned as partners together for approximately five years. She was a diligent worker, and together we put in an earnest effort to solve many felony cases. She was the type who kept me grounded and remained focused. We also became good friends and learned a lot about each other.

As a detective, I learned a great deal in a short time about how to collect evidence at a crime scene, process fingerprints, and conduct follow-up work, including interviewing witnesses and suspects.

In SPOT, I attended several interview schools and found that interviewing people came easily to me.

I investigated numerous home burglaries and thefts from vehicles. During my time in SPOT, the police chief awarded me thirteen Letters of Commendation for solving burglaries, recovering thousands of dollars' worth of stolen property, and returning it to the victims and owners.

Working Concerts

SPOT detectives were assigned to assist the narcotics unit during concerts at the Centroplex (now known as the Raising Cane's River Center). We also investigated potential car burglaries in the parking lot. We worked in pairs, so another SPOT detective was assigned to work with me. We teamed up and patrolled the Centroplex parking lots in plain clothes. We walked through the lots and open streets during the concerts, watching for individuals who might try to break into vehicles or linger around attempting to sell drugs.

We often encountered individuals attempting to break into parked cars, and we would walk right up to them in the process. We would ask what they were doing, and they would say they were trying to get into the vehicle because they wanted the radio or saw something else they wanted to steal. They had no clue who we were, and we would pretend as if we would help them. We actually sat back and watched them commit the burglary, and when they entered the vehicle by breaking the glass or using a tool to unlock it, we would watch them rip out the radio and ransack the vehicle.

When they came out of the vehicle, we would arrest them with our weapons drawn, then handcuff them, placing them under arrest. Afterward, we would call for a police unit to come to our area to pick up the offenders and transport them to jail for booking, along with the evidence they took.

I can't recall how many cases we solved by doing things like that on concert nights. My partner and I had a way of presenting ourselves that made it unlikely for anyone to suspect we were police. We would approach the bad guys, and they trusted us enough to ask for our help with something or even request a ride to their house to leave the scene.

Our most fun was going inside the Centroplex during a concert to work on drug cases. While in the arena, we walked around the facility looking for people selling, buying, or smoking drugs. We searched for anything from marijuana (a joint) to cocaine, and even Quaalude tablets. Yes, Quaaludes were prominent in the late seventies and early eighties. If my memory serves me right, they were $5 for each tablet.

We walked up and down the aisles inside the arena while the concert was ongoing. When we smelled marijuana burning, we would sit in an empty seat nearby to try to pinpoint the source of the smell until we saw someone smoking a marijuana joint. After identifying the source, we approached that individual and attempted to befriend them by asking for a hit off the joint. Dressed in plain clothes, they had no idea who we were, and most of the time, they were so high that they wouldn't think twice about handing us the joint. When that occurred, we would take the joint, and after ensuring no one else in the area was smoking, we would escort the person down to the police station in the building's basement. Once there, we would turn them and the joint (evidence) over to the duty officers for processing. Then we would return to the crowd to look for more drug violators.

While working undercover, we successfully confiscated a variety of drugs at concerts and arrested between fifteen and twenty individuals during the night.

After the concerts, we would investigate the arrested individuals and sometimes confiscate additional drugs from them, turning some of them into informants.

Honestly, there were nights during concerts when we were so busy making arrests that we had to decline opportunities to buy drugs from other individuals. There comes a time when you have to say enough is enough and call it a night. You can't arrest them all.

We were often assigned to provide security in the performers' stage area. In plain clothes, we would walk around the stage while also detecting narcotics on individuals and making numerous arrests. I have worked at many concerts and can't remember them all. However, some notable groups included Alabama, Foreigner, ZZ Top, Neil Diamond, Barry Manilow, Styx, Journey, Kansas, Boston, and many, many more.

I recall working near the stage area one night when the country band Alabama was set to perform. About two hours before the show began, they were in the Centroplex kitchen area on the bottom floor. I checked everything and saw the Alabama group members eating red beans and rice at a table. After chatting with them for a minute, I joined them for some red beans and rice. This was when Alabama started to gain popularity, but I didn't know much about their music or country music. I enjoyed meeting the band members and engaging in small talk, which prompted me to pay closer attention to their music, particularly country music.

Linda enjoyed country music and the group Alabama. She often attended country concerts at the Centroplex, and whenever a country band performed there, I would check with Linda to see if she wanted to go; if she did, I made sure she could enjoy the concert. Typically, she brought along her friend from Denham Springs, Sherri Breaux, and I had no issues getting them both into the venue. They both thoroughly enjoyed it.

On many occasions, I could take them down near the stage area where I worked security and let them stand there to watch the concert. Those were fun times for Linda and me as we enjoyed watching the concerts while I worked. However, I didn't invite her to heavy rock concerts because I knew I would be working on narcotics cases. Besides, Linda was uninterested in heavy metal concerts and never attended them.

Special Assignment to Narcotics

On February 4, 1980, I received notice of a temporary assignment (detail) to the BRPD narcotics unit, as I was relatively new and not well-known in the city. I was tasked with conducting undercover operations, seeking out and purchasing narcotics from specific known targets. The detail was scheduled to last until approximately April 1, 1980.

After settling into the narcotics unit, I collaborated with several other narcotics detectives who had been assigned there for some time. They were still able to work undercover, and their identities were never compromised. I worked most closely with two specific narcotics detectives with whom I had previously worked. Together, we managed numerous undercover cases in various adult clubs throughout the northern Baton Rouge area and East Baton Rouge Parish.

One day, the BRPD Intelligence Unit notified us that they had received significant information about various types of narcotics being distributed through nightclubs, strip clubs, and similar establishments in northern Baton Rouge. After receiving the complete information, the lieutenant in charge of narcotics assigned me the task. I was to visit all of those establishments, make friends, and flash some money in front of people to create an impression.

We soon began frequenting those clubs and bars to start our assignment, and after a few weeks, the dancers and bar workers recognized us for spending money at the establishments. After establishing trust and a good rapport, we convinced them to introduce us to people they knew who sold drugs around the venues. The drugs ranged from cocaine and marijuana to Quaaludes and other illegal substances. However, there was more to it than simply getting them to introduce us to their drug dealers.

As I mentioned, the process involved building trust and forming friendships with everyone we engaged with; this required time, resources, and money. However, if you are successful, it is worth it because it pays off. When I mentioned it took time, I referred to weeks or months of visiting the same location frequently to strengthen our presence.

After a month or two, we befriended some dancers and bartenders. Then, we started receiving invitations to parties and outings where we could potentially meet someone who might sell us drugs. At this point, you feel a sense of pride building up, which motivates you to develop a case. Your time and effort are not wasted.

Now, we had ways to help motivate those willing to help us. One little trick we used while working was the use of lidocaine powder, which is a medical numbing agent. When we befriended one of the dancers and started discussing cocaine, we would invite them out to our vehicle. There, we showed them this little vial containing the white lidocaine powder, telling them that it was cocaine.

We kept it in a small vial because, at that time, that was how cocaine was typically carried. We would lay some of the lidocaine out on a small mirror, lining it up for them to snort through their noses. Then we took a dollar bill and rolled it up to use like a straw. When it started to numb their noses (like cocaine would do), they would honestly believe it was pure cocaine. They even began to act as if they were getting high from it.

At this point, I would do everything I could to keep from laughing because if they only knew how silly they were, snorting lidocaine and believing they were getting high! None of them knew the difference or even questioned us about what we gave them. As far as they knew, we were providing them with free cocaine, and they loved it. That also shows how desperate these ladies were for the drug.

We only carried a small amount with us for a reason. When our little portion was used up, they would want more, and we had to explain that it was all we had. We would then ask them if they knew anyone willing to sell us some cocaine. Unbelievably, it worked nearly every time; they would tell us to wait until they got off work so they could take us to their dealer.

Of course, we would hang out, and around 2:00 a.m., after the club closed, the dancer(s) would meet us in the parking lot and take us to a location—whether a house, restaurant, or even a playground—to purchase drugs. Sometimes, they rode with us; other times, we followed them. If we followed them, it meant they were staying or living at that location. If they wanted to ride with us, we knew it was a random location.

When we arrived at the location, we were introduced as friends from the club looking to purchase drugs. They typically escorted us to the dealer, but we often had to go through an intermediary who represented the dealer.

Occasionally, upon reaching a location, we were instructed to remain in the car while they entered to purchase drugs on our behalf with our funds. During their absence, we documented the address and described the site for future reference. The quantity of information they inadvertently gave us was remarkable, and we later shared that intelligence with the narcotics division for search warrant purposes.

We frequently visited various locations and met with the dealers, which was fantastic! This approach enabled us to build our relationships with them. Eventually, we could involve other narcotic agents by connecting them together. This would allow us to keep making purchases until we chose to arrest the dealer. Moreover, by the time other agents carried out the arrest, we would have distanced ourselves from the dealer so that they wouldn't suspect us at all.

Our method proved effective, enabling us to manage numerous narcotic cases. Nevertheless, we faced challenges in establishing connections since not everything operated flawlessly. Yet, we persisted, learned from our errors, and refined our technique.

Because we worked undercover, once we purchased any drugs or evidence, we would turn it and any information we obtained over to a narcotic "top agent." A top agent was an agent who wasn't undercover and could draft reports for us and acquire whatever we needed, eliminating the need for us to go to the narcotics office. Working this way protected us from potentially blowing our cover, and the top agents would take our information and evidence to obtain arrest warrants and/or search warrants, furthering our investigation.

Even though people eventually discovered that the dealers they introduced us to had been arrested, they never made the connection that we were involved. We consistently remained safe and unnoticed. Often, those same individuals would take us back to the very dealers who had been apprehended, enabling us to buy more drugs from them, which would result in new charges later on. Eventually, the dealer would "wake up," often blaming other acquaintances for informing the police. They never honestly suspected us to be law enforcement and would even invite us to the weekend parties they organized. We continually operated unnoticed among the criminals, as they never suspected us; I like to believe we excelled at our roles.

Don't think we were naïve about the drug dealers we befriended; we always kept in mind that the drug dealers were merely playing us after they were arrested.

When the dealer accused others of reporting them to the police, we had to take precautions to protect ourselves and those who were inadvertently helping us, ensuring that nothing tragic would happen to them. Some drug dealers could easily erase someone from the face of the earth for revenge. If we felt it was becoming too dangerous for the person inadvertently assisting us, we would have them arrested and removed from the streets for their safety. The top agent making the arrest would explain the situation to them. Remember, there would already be an arrest warrant for them due to their involvement in leading us to their dealers. Also, keep in mind that initially, they were the ones who arranged the narcotic purchases with their dealers in the first place. They were not saints by any means.

Now, doing all this was fine, but we still had to worry about ourselves and each other. Once drug dealers were arrested, they could become extremely cautious and paranoid, often beginning to suspect everyone of turning against them. They would still take chances selling their drugs because the money was too good, and they got to play the role of the "big dog" to everyone.

As the "big dogs," they believed that people respected them, but there was no genuine respect involved, as everyone wanted their drugs, no matter what or how they would get them. Being a "big dog" to most people who were purchasing meant nothing at all.

Still, every time we visited one of the dealers, we remained overly cautious and had a plan ready in case something went wrong during our time with them. One never knew what was going through their minds, and establishing trust proved to be difficult.

Not All Goes Right

I noted that you put in great effort to ensure everything runs smoothly without errors. Understand your background, have a backup plan, and put in the effort, but recognize that sometimes things can go awry.

One night, we were preparing to execute a search warrant on a known drug dealer's residence. We staged at the narcotics office, and after developing our game plan, we broke off into teams and loaded up in several vans to go to the residence.

I was riding in the back of the lead van along with numerous other agents. Our job was to pull directly up to the residence, jump out, and go to the front door, announcing our arrival. If necessary, we would break down the door. Great plan!

As we drove up to the target's residence, the van slowed down and prepared to stop so we could exit the vehicle. We were in the back and knew that as soon as the van stopped, we would swing open the door and jump out. The van stopped, the door slid open, and another officer and I attempted to leap out when the van took off and threw us into a residential yard.

While lying on the ground and gazing up, I noticed the van had pulled up two houses away and come to a halt. By the time we managed to lift ourselves off the ground and gather our equipment to reach the house, the agents had already entered.

As we approached, the other agents inquired about our whereabouts. Naturally, they were aware of our location and chuckled about it for a while.

Honestly, it wasn't my fault. But that's how things can go wrong quickly. Luckily, I only had a bruised ego, but it healed swiftly. During the subsequent search warrant I participated in, I made sure to ride in a different van.

Another incident occurred involving me and one of my partners during an undercover buy-bust mission. This mission aimed to befriend a specific target and subsequently purchase drugs from him. We would then arrest him immediately and enlist him as an informant for the narcotics unit.

My partner and I walked into this place in North Baton Rouge and pinpointed our target. We took our time, gradually getting to know him and building a connection. We played pool and bought him a few drinks, and as the night progressed, discussions about drugs came up. Thankfully, he offered to take us to his house to "party" with him and some friends who would be present. Our original goal was to buy drugs off him there and then lure him outside to make the arrest. But now, we had to leave the premises and go to his house, where a party was going to happen.

Outside the establishment, several other agents were

watching and waiting for us to emerge with the target and make the arrest. They were our surveillance team. As I said, the original goal was for us not to leave the establishment because we didn't have enough agents to conduct proper surveillance and follow us anywhere. While talking with this target, he spoke about how much marijuana he had at his house, along with some cocaine, and suggested we could all have a big party. Now, he wanted to charge us up front for some of the drugs, and we were willing to do so once we were there and saw what he had. Sometimes it's called good-faith money; they want to see how real you were about buying, and the thought was that if we paid some now, then we couldn't be cops. Yeah, right! That reminds me that at one time, the word on the street was that if you are asked three times if you are a cop and you reply no, then they can't be arrested. I believe drugs have a way of manipulating the mind, making you believe all sorts of stupid things.

Anyway, we exited the establishment, and my partner and I tried to get the attention of our surveillance team to inform them that we were leaving with the target. Honestly, I thought they had seen us and followed us to the residence, so we were good to go.

We rode in the target's vehicle for several minutes, making turns left and right, navigating up and down the street, turning around, and heading back to where we came from. We then drove down more streets until he finally stopped. I had forgotten to mention that I drove. I convinced the target that he was too impaired to drive, and that I liked his car, so he let me drive.

When we arrived, we parked, got out, and slowly walked into the target's residence. This should have given our surveillance team time to catch up to us and watch us enter the target's house. As far as we knew, we were good to go.

We entered the house, and at any given moment, there were seven to eight people in the room coming and going. After a few drinks, the target revealed some of his drugs, which included several pounds of marijuana, a bag of assorted pain pills, and a small amount of cocaine. Keep in mind, it was just me and my partner against everyone else in that room. I stood on one side, while my partner was on the other. We didn't want to be on the same side of the room; if any shooting started, we could return fire from different angles. We positioned ourselves to ensure we were not in each other's line of fire.

As the drugs were laid out on a coffee table, I looked at my partner, and he gave me a nod, meaning let's take it all down before people started using some of it. We drew our weapons and badges, shouting for everyone to lie on the floor. Panic started immediately. Everyone started running and then fighting, kicking, and shoving each other. While chaos ensued among them, my partner and I stood there watching them. Yes, they were fighting each other. My partner and I ended up standing against the wall, watching them fight. What in the hell was going on? After a few minutes of watching them beat the crap out of each other, we finally had to put a halt to it. Someone was going to get badly hurt if we didn't.

We finally got everything settled down, and everyone was now on the floor on their bellies with their hands behind their backs. My partner opened the front door and stuck his head out, waving for our surveillance team to come in and assist us.

Well, we waited several minutes, but no one arrived. So, where was our surveillance team? With everyone on the floor and my partner's weapon drawn, I grabbed the house phone and called our headquarters dispatch. I told the dispatcher who I was and that I needed to notify our surveillance team to come inside. When the dispatcher contacted our surveillance team, they were lost and did not know where we were located. They were looking for the vehicle that we left in. The dispatcher asked me for the address, and she would send them to us. I said okay, but then my mind went blank. Where are we? I didn't know the address where we were. I had to put dispatch on hold and go into the room and get the target off the floor to ask him for the address. Surprisingly, he cooperated and gave me the address to provide dispatch. A few minutes later, the surveillance team arrived.

As it turned out, one of the surveillance team members was the driver of the van that threw me into the front yard during that search warrant event. We laughed it off, but it shows how quickly dangerous situations can escalate. We thought we were under surveillance, and help was just outside the door. But in fact, my partner and I were alone, taking down eight people in a small house filled with drugs. Yet, we did it!

Stories such as these happen constantly; you learn from them and hope they don't occur again. But they always do.

A significant error arises from becoming overly complacent. On one occasion, I needed to check out a bar in West Baton Rouge but hadn't thoroughly finished my homework. My assignment was to visit the bar, observe, and listen for a while to see if anything noteworthy was occurring or if any known drug dealers frequented the venue. After entering, I took a seat at the bar, and about an hour later, I noticed several men keeping an eye on me. Each time I moved to a different spot in the bar, they followed me closely, watching.

Not long after moving for the third time, I was confronted, and one accused me of ratting to the police on one of their friends. They didn't call me a cop, just a rat. Well, it ended up being four of them who grabbed me and "walked" me outside the bar. Good, I assumed they would walk me to my car and tell me to leave, which I would have been happy to do.

Well, I felt the first blow to the mid-portion of my back, and then several more followed. I immediately fell to the ground to help protect myself, and that's when the kicking started. Apparently, they were too fat and lazy to reach down and punch me. I don't believe there was a spot on my body that didn't get kicked at least once.

Finally, they dragged me to a ditch out by the highway in front of the bar and dumped me in it. I can assure you I had had enough, so I lay there for a while and didn't move. I was hoping they thought I was hurt enough and would leave me alone. I noticed that they walked over to their vehicles, and all four left the premises, leaving me in the ditch, which, don't get me wrong, I was okay with. I thanked them as they drove off.

I had to find a way to get up. No one could spot me, and I realized that if I didn't act, no one else would help me. I somehow managed to crawl out of the ditch and made my way to my vehicle. The night was cool, and I was slightly damp, but I couldn't decide if the cold and wetness bothered me more than the aches and pains from being punched and kicked. Eventually, I was able to drive to the narcotics office and received some assistance there. If you know me, there's no way

I was going to a hospital. That is a sign of weakness, and I wasn't giving them the satisfaction. I was going to let them know that they didn't hurt me. But, oh man, was I hurting…

Long story short, I was able to identify them because I knew about two of them, and we later arrested all four. After talking with them, I turned two of them into informants for me, and they provided plenty of information that led to numerous drug arrests. The funny thing is, they ended up giving me information about the very person they had originally beaten me up over.

Over time, the two guys became decent friends of mine. It's funny how certain things turn out. Neither of them had an arrest record to begin with, and they ended up with probation for what they did to me. The other two received six months each, and they spent every day in jail. But I lived to fight another day! All in a day's work because it wasn't the first time, and I knew it wouldn't be the last.

Surveillance on Victims

We defined a victim as anyone we were familiar with who used drugs, an informant hired to buy narcotics, or even individuals who unwittingly helped us obtain narcotics, like dancers or club staff.

Sometimes, we took it upon ourselves to surveil these

people to see what they were doing and, at times, to keep them safe. Conducting surveillance on a victim (a known user of narcotics) wasn't a popular tactic, but it proved effective on many occasions.

When we began tracking these victims, we could identify where three or more dealers lived and who was responsible for most of the drug sales. Of course, the only way we observed these dealers was by covertly following the victims, allowing them to lead us directly to the dealers' homes. We then verified the addresses and vehicle license plates to ascertain who resided there, their places of employment, and the ownership of the vehicles. This provided a wealth of intelligence for future cases.

By tracking the victim, we were able to identify a dealer and occasionally observed a drug deal in progress. This ultimately led to the arrest of both the victim and the dealer, resulting in felony convictions.

The victims we surveyed were unaware of our surveillance. They may have recently been released from jail, just bonded out, or never been arrested, but we had reasonable suspicion that they were users. These victims would take us to houses, restaurants, or other locations while meeting with potential dealers or users to make purchases.

When the victim met someone in a parked car, we obtained

the license plate information and vehicle type; often, we had a camera to photograph the incident. We gathered all this information, returned to the office, and conducted investigative research. Sometimes, when we checked the person the victim met, we found that they almost always had a record of a narcotics arrest. We collected all this information and provided it to our intelligence division. There are numerous ways to develop potential criminal cases for both the suspect and the victim.

A good example is the following case. After identifying the suspect with whom the victim had met, I followed that suspect to a local bar. I went inside and found a way to befriend him while sitting at the bar. After making contact and talking with him for a while, I built trust with him, and we began discussing drugs, the police, and other topics.

After a while, I mentioned the "victim's" name to him, explaining that the victim was a friend of mine who was supposed to bring me some weed (marijuana), but it hadn't gone through yet. The suspect asked me how I knew the victim, and I had a fabricated cover story that the suspect believed was true. Eventually, the suspect said he could take care of me with some weed, and he took me to his house. Yes, I know, what a fool he was. Now, this didn't work every time, but on occasions, we scored!

Upon arriving at his home, we talked for a while, and I could tell he was starting to trust me more because he revealed his entire stash of drugs hidden in his house. I told him I would take some of the weed off his hands, but I had a friend who would also take some of the cocaine he had. I ended up making a small purchase of marijuana from him while I was inside his house. We talked for a while afterward, and I could tell I had his trust, and he was trying to become a friend of mine.

A few days later, I brought in a different undercover narcotics agent and made the introductions. This new agent bought more drugs from the dealer multiple times. The new agent worked so well with the dealer that the dealer connected him with another dealer friend to enable larger transactions. What a world! It's all about money!

Over the course of ten months, we initiated thirty-two felony cases against the primary dealer and filed additional cases for larger transactions. By larger transactions, I refer to instances involving more than 50 pounds of marijuana on two occasions and over half a pound of cocaine. Both dealers were sentenced to over ten years in prison.

Many dealers invited me to their drug parties, and whenever I received an invitation to a dealer's home for a gathering, I always asked if I could bring a date; naturally, they would agree. I would then bring a female narcotics agent as my date to the party. Instead of one of us being present, we now had two agents working the party.

At these events, we were able to meet numerous drug dealers and users, and the "higher" they were, the easier it became for us to do our job: obtaining intelligence for future cases.

From a party we attended, we arranged months of intelligence and drug purchases that eventually led to over twenty people being criminally arrested and "a lot" of drugs seized. This was all accomplished by building trust. The main problem we encountered while attending parties was running into someone who might know one of us.

At parties, you constantly scan the room, taking mental notes of everyone present and cross-checking with your partner to ensure everything is clear. Even when a new person arrived at the party, you needed to recheck to confirm that the person was trustworthy and that you had never met them before. The goal was for you and your partner to find just one individual who was willing to leave the party with you and take you somewhere to purchase drugs. Your main goal was to do your job and go home alive. Keep in mind that some of these dealers wouldn't think twice about "getting rid" of you if needed. If it were between their money and going to jail or eliminating you, it would be you. The best thing you could pray for was to let it be quick. But it wouldn't be, I can assure you.

Establishing trust was important, but we only consumed beverages from cans or fresh bottles. I also limited my eating; if I noticed someone eating something without adverse effects, I might consider trying it. The last thing anyone wanted was to get drugged unknowingly.

The objective was to explore a new area and expand our network to identify additional locations, addresses, and people. It is essential to note that there can never be too many drug cases to manage or dealers to apprehend.

Although I knew of the consequences, I felt proud of my actions, immersing myself among criminals, sometimes for months, to help catch a bad guy. Performing all of this work paid off in the courtroom when the bad guy was sentenced.

Store Watch

While working in narcotics, I cultivated creative thinking and a keen interest in discovering new methods for apprehending criminals. In areas of the city where drug trafficking was rampant and arrests were frequent, it became essential to step back and approach the situation with creativity, particularly when narcotic intelligence indicated a significant crime presence. Taking action was imperative.

One day, while working on several burglary cases, my

partner and I rode through a high-narcotics crime area in North Baton Rouge. We were not assigned to narcotics at the time and were focused on burglary cases. However, when things were slow or we encountered a narcotics case, supervisors from SPOT or the Narcotics Unit didn't mind if we handled it, as long as we kept our supervisor informed.

As we rode through a particularly high-crime area, I began to think that when dealers prepare to sell marijuana, they need baggies to separate the marijuana for easier sales. Dealers take a pound of marijuana and break it down into smaller amounts for simpler selling on the street. Back then, they called it nickel or dime bags. What are nickel or dime bags? As you may have heard, these terms are frequently mentioned in TV shows and other media, but what exactly do these slang terms mean? Well, a nickel bag is a small bag of marijuana that costs $5 (a nickel bag). It is typically enough weed to roll several joints, and, of course, a $10 bag (a dime bag).

As I stated above, dealers often package small amounts of marijuana in plastic bags and sell them at low prices to appeal to a broader customer base. The terms "nickel bag" and "dime bag" of weed quickly caught on and became common ways to refer to this specific quantity of weed.

Today, these terms are seldom used. I recently spoke with the local police in my hometown and asked them about the terms "nickel" and "dime bags." I was told that these terms are not used much these days, and it was also mentioned that with the legalization and decriminalization of marijuana in many places, the idea of a standardized price for a specific amount of weed has become less relevant.

As my partner and I explored the area, I found myself contemplating where to purchase sandwich bags for packaging marijuana for sale. Surprisingly, the answer was a grocery store. We drove through a region notorious for drug trafficking, and I decided to stop at a supermarket in North Baton Rouge. Although it wasn't very large, they had sandwich bags available.

The store was bustling with customers, so I told my partner I'd go inside for a bit and observe the baggie aisle to see if anyone would make a purchase. After we exited the vehicle, I picked up a shopping cart to blend in as a shopper.

While we were watching the aisle where the baggies were located, it wasn't long before I noticed two young white males walking down the aisle of baggies directly in front of me. I pretended to be shopping as I observed them, and they conversed under their breath before both began grabbing handfuls of assorted-sized baggie boxes. Now, I wondered why they needed so many boxes of baggies? Ha! I knew.

After grabbing all the boxes they could carry, they walked toward the checkout line without purchasing anything else.

Watching them go through the checkout, I saw they bought approximately fifteen boxes of assorted baggie sizes. I followed them outside as they gathered their bags and exited the store.

Before they could enter their vehicle, my partner and I approached them and identified ourselves as police officers. They stood there with all those boxes of baggies, both wearing a "deer in the headlights" expression. This was around noon; their eyes were bloodshot, and both appeared to be flying high as a kite.

I started talking with them, spinning a story that we had been watching them both for some time under surveillance and, based on information from others, we knew they had marijuana stashed away, ready for sale. I explained that by buying all the baggies, we knew they were preparing to process the marijuana for sale. I told them that by purchasing the baggies, they had committed an overt act in a criminal conspiracy by buying baggies to separate the marijuana for sale. Please don't read too much into what I said because I made it up. It just came to me, so I went with it. You should have seen my partner's face when I said it.

After sharing this story, I explained that if they were willing to cooperate, provide information, and surrender their marijuana, we wouldn't have to execute a search warrant on their homes, tearing everything apart in search of it.

My partner ran a record check to see if they had an arrest record, and neither had any prior arrests. We identified the two as being twenty-one and twenty-two years old. Trust me when I say they were as dumb as a bag of rocks or just "high."

One of the males immediately stated that he lived with his parents and didn't want them to know about anything. The other male mentioned he stayed at his friend's house and was just there to help. I informed them both that if they cooperated with us and surrendered the marijuana, we could work to protect them as long as they cooperated with us.

Eventually, they took us to both of their houses, where we recovered approximately ten pounds of marijuana and fifty Quaalude tablets from each location. Although there was still more, we had enough to establish our case and develop them into informants for future use.

When we finally got it together, we wrote the reports and officially documented the two males as our new informants. We let them go for the time being, and they were profoundly grateful, but they knew we would call on them later. With these two now helping us, we could make many more narcotic cases, as they introduced us to numerous drug dealers.

By meeting these drug dealers, we were able to bring in other undercover agents to conduct controlled narcotic purchases and even consider introducing more agents into the cases.

We worked these two men hard for about seven months, building many narcotic cases. However, a time came when we had to reel it all in and arrest them for the original drug charges (from the grocery store incident). They had to pay the price, but they received some leniency because they assisted us with numerous other narcotic cases. The two were put on probation and were not sentenced to jail time. Still, the judge ordered them to undergo drug rehabilitation and not to be caught again with drugs or to associate with anyone linked to narcotics. Let's face it, that was a good deal for those two knuckleheads.

You must admit that working the store watch was a great idea, and I employed that technique numerous times with remarkable success. I'm sorry my technique didn't catch on with the other agents because they claimed it took too much time. I tried many times to explain that the payoff would be significant with patience, but some agents were unwilling to wait. That's all I'll say about that. It was their loss; I did pretty well making cases and felony arrests.

I mentioned "controlled buys" several times, so let me briefly explain what that term means. A controlled buy is a type of drug investigation where I purchase narcotics, but first, other officers search me to confirm that I have no contraband (drugs) on me. Then, I receive money that is recorded or documented by serial numbers to use for the purchase. I am then transported to a prearranged location to complete my transaction with the individual.

After the purchase, the suspect is immediately arrested, and the money used is confiscated. The money matches the documented serial numbers, meaning the suspect has police money, and I possess the product (drugs). It is difficult to challenge this scenario in court.

Remember that the police arrange controlled narcotic purchases through an undercover agent or occasionally a confidential informant in a similar way. Now you're informed!

Stabbed in the Right Knee

Often, detectives from the SPOT and narcotics units would gather to conduct operations or sweep the streets. As a group, we would visit city areas and observe people spending time on street corners. We would stop to approach these individuals for identification purposes and check for outstanding warrants or if they had drugs on their person. If they had a warrant, we would arrest them and take them to the station for processing. Sometimes, we found drugs on their person, but most of the time, we discovered drugs lying on the street where they were standing.

Of course, they would know nothing about it or its

origin. I wondered if everyone on the corner was named "Who me?" because when you ask them for their name, "Who me?" responds. Sometimes, they would ask who we were looking for, and we would reply that we were looking for the dude on the corner. Whenever we arrested someone with stolen merchandise and asked where they got it, the answer was always "the dude on the corner." So, we were always looking for that dude on the corner.

On March 29, 1984, at 8:20 p.m., during a group operation, we operated in the 1400 block of Thomas Delpit Street, aiming to arrest multiple individuals for narcotic violations and other offenses.

I encountered a Black male standing alone, whom we later identified, who reeked of a strong odor of marijuana. I began speaking with him to determine his identity. I informed him that I was going to conduct a body search, and when I started searching for weapons and illegal drugs, he refused to cooperate and attempted to leave the area by walking away from me. I stopped him, placed him under arrest, and he started assaulting me by punching me in the head, neck, and back while trying to escape. I held onto him, and we began to fight. When I turned him upside down, I was holding his legs in the air while his hands were near my legs. I was preparing to throw him to the side when I felt a sharp pain in the center of my right knee, causing me to fall to the ground with him lying on top of me. The pain was extreme, and I was going in and out of consciousness.

At one point, I woke up to find other agents staring at me while I lay on the ground.

While lying there, I heard the faint sound of an ambulance siren, and I was later transported to Baton Rouge General Hospital, where they identified a deep puncture wound in my right knee. At that time, I felt no sensation from my knee down to my foot. When I attempted to stand, I was unable to control my right leg and couldn't bear any weight on my foot.

I met with Dr. Steven Wilson, an orthopedic surgeon who performed surgery on my knee. He discovered that the tendons were severed and required complete repair. After the surgery, I stayed in the hospital for a few days before being discharged to go home. It took months for my knee to heal, and eventually, I returned to work in the narcotics unit.

Also, that night, the officers at the scene arrested the individual and charged him accordingly. However, he later pleaded guilty to lesser charges and was released on probation.

Commendations

Just a brief moment to brag. While in SPOT, I received twenty-two commendation letters from the Chief of Police for my work in conducting investigations leading to arrests and the recovery of stolen property.

Permanent Transfer to Narcotics

On July 23, 1984, I was permanently moved to the Narcotics Unit. Initially, I was instructed to continue working as an undercover agent and adhere to my established methods.

Working undercover, I had several identifications using a driver's license and other documents. There were times when I needed to officially change my undercover name after completing cases. I had to obtain a new undercover identity with a driver's license and additional documentation under that name. Additionally, I had to create a new backstory for my new self to facilitate conversations with drug dealers and informants. This required a story that I could memorize and incorporate into my life, including details about where I was born, where I attended school, and where I had lived and worked in the past.

When developing a backstory, it's essential to have supporting information. For example, if I claimed I was born in New Orleans, I would follow up by saying I lived on Dumaine Street near Bayou St. John, close to the City Park gate. Therefore, it's essential to learn the area and its significant points of interest. This way, if anyone is familiar with the location, it should convince them that I truly hail from New Orleans. The same applies to employment, but don't claim to be an electrician if you know nothing about the trade. Be smart.

My assigned undercover partner was someone I had previously worked with on numerous narcotics cases. We worked effectively together, and eventually, our wives became friends.

As for the work, nothing changed, and I continued as before, just permanently. I had just gotten a new partner, and as always happens when you get a new partner, you need to learn each other's dos and don'ts, likes and dislikes, and, most importantly, develop trust.

Partners working in narcotics must share a specific bond and be able to trust one another because our lives depend on it. I needed to know that my partner would be there for me when things went sour, and he needed to know the same. We eventually developed that relationship very quickly and became best friends.

Marijuana "Trees"

Other law enforcement agencies frequently requested our assistance with their narcotics cases. At times, they would ask for an undercover agent, hoping that no one in their area would recognize the agent. However, whenever a request came in, the chief made every effort to provide them with assistance.

My partner and I assisted the Livingston Parish Sheriff's Office in a drug case. They requested help from the BRPD, and our supervisor assigned my partner and me to aid in their investigation.

We ultimately met with the Livingston deputies for an intelligence briefing. They reported that two men were supposedly cultivating marijuana plants in their backyard at the same residence. The deputies mentioned that they had tried to locate the plants but were unsuccessful.

According to the information received, the two men were reportedly cultivating marijuana in a specific area of their backyard heavily covered with brush, making it difficult to see. The deputies indicated that the house was located off the interstate, and while the backyard was partially visible, visibility was limited.

Initially, the deputies suggested that we wear state workers' vests and approach the backyard, pretending to work in hopes of spotting the plants. However, the rear area was heavily guarded by brush, rendering it challenging to view the entire backyard from the interstate.

After our intelligence briefing concluded, we devised a plan to sneak into the back of the property located between the interstate and the suspect's backyard. We disagreed with the state workers' proposal and decided to conduct our surveillance at night. The only route to see into the backyard involved entering from the interstate and walking through the wooded area toward the back of the suspect's house.

We entered close to the suspect's property when it got dark, taking cover behind some brush and small trees. From there, we began watching the property and waited for most of the night, surveying the area. We wanted to see if anyone would appear on the property during the night.

After searching the area visually without success, we went back to the bushes and small trees where we intended to remain hidden until daylight.

As we waited for daylight, the wind began to pick up, and a strong smell of marijuana enveloped us. Familiar with that scent, we struggled to identify its source. We intended to leave the brush at dawn to meet the Livingston deputies and share our observations. Before departing, we deliberated on what to inform the deputies since no marijuana plants had been found. Despite the unmistakable smell in the air, the origin of the odor remained unknown to us.

Daylight was arriving, and we were preparing to leave the area to head toward where the deputies would be waiting for us. I grabbed one of the small trees we had been sitting under to pull myself up, and as I rose, I smelled a strong odor of marijuana around my head. When I looked up, I realized we were standing among approximately twenty or more tall marijuana "trees." These marijuana trees stood about ten to twelve feet tall, and upon seeing them, we started laughing. The marijuana trees were not on the suspects' property but on state-owned property. That was one reason we didn't discover them. Initially, we searched all around the backyard area and never thought to check back at the state property. Although we could smell the marijuana, we didn't see it.

We later discovered that the suspects admitted they had deliberately planted the marijuana there to avoid putting it on their property. During the investigation and interview process with the two individuals, they confessed to planting the marijuana plants, and the Livingston Sheriff's Office charged them both accordingly. Subsequently, they pleaded guilty to the charges.

We cut down a marijuana tree and took it along to show the deputies what we discovered. They were astonished that we found the plants so quickly. One deputy asked why we had taken so long to report after spotting the trees, and I explained that we had waited to see if anyone would return to check on them. We couldn't reveal how we located the trees; that would have been too embarrassing. Ultimately, all the marijuana plants were removed and destroyed.

Over time, my partner and I worked on many more narcotics cases together, as well as various other cases, including prostitution, purchasing stolen property, and buying stolen cars. I can share many funny stories about our work on prostitution cases, but I will save those for another time. We continued to work together at the Centroplex concerts, walking through the crowds, buying drugs, and making arrests.

I'm not bragging, but I was pretty successful in purchasing drugs and building solid criminal narcotics cases. Upon request, I worked on numerous criminal cases with the Louisiana State Police and various law enforcement agencies.

Wellness Check

Before I left the narcotics unit in the summer of 1985, the police department was extremely busy managing a crime spree and a significant number of rapes. Murders were also rising, and the department was shorthanded with too few detectives to handle the influx.

At times, detectives from narcotics and burglary were assigned to support homicide units and reduce their caseload.

One afternoon, while responding to a wellness check, I was dispatched to an apartment building where neighbors had complained of an overpowering odor emanating from one of the third-floor apartments. Upon arrival, I met the complainant, who led me up the stairs toward the apartment.

However, when we reached the second floor, I started to smell the odor and immediately recognized it: the unmistakable scent of a deceased body. By the time we reached the locked apartment door, the smell had become nearly unbearable, so I instructed the manager to unlock it. After he unlocked and opened the door, the manager began vomiting, which caused the complainant to vomit as well. Thus, I was now contending with the unbearable smell coming from the apartment and two men standing next to me, retching in the hallway.

I walked into the apartment and headed toward the bedroom, seeing nothing in the kitchen or living area. I began to hear the sound of flies coming from the bedroom, and when I looked inside, I found them swarming the bed. I then observed a body lying on the bed, with a pillow over the face. Assessing the scene, I immediately called the coroner's office and uniformed officers to assist with a potential crime scene, as I couldn't determine whether it was a suicide or a homicide.

Later, several uniformed officers arrived at the scene, one of whom was a newcomer who had recently graduated from the academy. I examined the area and determined that the individual died of natural causes. There was no evidence of a crime scene. We later learned it was an elderly man with cancer.

When the coroner arrived, he pronounced the individual

deceased and instructed that the body be taken to the morgue for an autopsy. When one of the coroner's staff came to transport the body, I had the rookie officer walk into the bedroom with me while he tried not to vomit, as his face had already taken on various shades of color. I had previously spoken with the coroner's staff and informed them of my plans, and they laughed, stepping back to wait for me to finish. Understand that the body had been deceased for many days and had swollen to the point where it was difficult to identify. The coroner's staff recognized that the moment they started to transport the body, it would burst, and you wouldn't want to be standing there when it did. The smell and bodily fluids would go everywhere and wouldn't be a pretty sight.

I asked the rookie officer to retrieve the pillow from the body and place it in an evidence bag for me. As soon as he reached the body and was grabbing for the pillowcase, the deceased's belly shook and burst. That rookie officer learned several lessons. First, never listen to me again, and second, when a body is in that state, you stay back and let the coroner's staff handle it because they are better equipped for those situations. The good news is that the rookie got over it, and we often laughed about it when we met each other elsewhere.

Chapter 6

Working Undercover

When I joined the BRPD, I knew I would arrest criminals and drug dealers, but I never believed I would have to portray one myself. While working undercover, I posed as a drug dealer, pretending to sell cocaine, marijuana, and various other types of narcotics.

On several occasions, I acted as a weapons dealer and a domestic terrorist, importing drugs and weapons from outside the country. I must admit that I became a skilled criminal during that time, but I also quickly learned how to lie and invent false stories at a moment's notice. I learned to deceive criminals so well that I occasionally began to believe some of it myself.

As I mentioned earlier, the undercover classes were suitable for a classroom environment, allowing you to learn and understand a great deal. The real lessons and life experiences came during actual work on the job. When bad guys surround you, if they know or find out you are a police officer, you are done. They would prefer to take you out once they feel betrayed by you. That's right, betrayed. When you build the trust and confidence of drug dealers, they don't handle betrayal very well.

Working in SPOT and Narcotics, I attended several interview and interrogation schools, as well as undercover classes. I was taught how to fabricate stories (lie) and create backstories for the characters I portrayed in class. However, nothing prepared me better for the art of deception and storytelling than being directly involved in the criminal aspect itself—in other words, pretending to be a criminal to the extent that I became a criminal in my mind. Working on criminal narcotic cases in the field was where I truly learned how to survive (stay alive) and maintain my character to complete my cases.

Often, it wasn't the quantity of drugs you purchased, but rather your ability to lie that could help you escape dangerous situations.

Working undercover required constant training from the FBI, the Louisiana State Police, and the East Baton Rouge Sheriff's Office. This training involved the same material repeated regularly, but it served as a valuable reminder.

Over time, I mastered the art of deception, covert hypnosis, and reading body language, but the best "school" I ever attended was working on the streets. You can sit in a classroom all day, but you must take that knowledge, apply it in the real world, and refine your techniques. However, many officers struggled to adapt to this way of life and eventually returned to their regular police duties, leaving the undercover world behind. There was no shame in this, as not everyone was cut out for that work.

Preparing for Undercover Work

I discussed the undercover operations I participated in, but it's essential to understand that they involve more than simply stating you will work undercover. As a case unfolds, numerous elements must be taken into account.

What are the objectives of these undercover operations, considering the various types of undercover work? How long is the operation expected to last? Will it involve a buy-bust scenario, or will you merely display a stack of cash to lure out the drugs?

Who will be tasked with undercover operations for this specific case? Choosing the right person for the undercover role is crucial. It's important for everyone to understand the risks involved in going undercover in this context.

Are you using a confidential informant? If so, is the undercover agent aware of the informant's history and cover story?

The undercover agent must develop a believable false identity and generate supporting evidence. While working undercover, it's crucial to remain authentic; steer clear of acting like someone or something you're not.

As an undercover agent, you need to know the target(s), necessitating familiarity with their criminal and personal backgrounds.

You should understand the importance of your appearance by selecting clothing that aligns with both your role and the status of the target(s) you are going to meet.

Planning, coordinating operations, and providing briefings are essential. Will the undercover agent be armed or unarmed, and has a decision been reached about using a wire for the undercover meeting? The undercover agent must maintain complete control over the operation, ensuring they can effectively manage the target(s). Monitoring is vital to protect the undercover agent. Who will take on this responsibility?

Supervisors should identify the appropriate moment to halt the operation, extract the undercover agent, and conclude the operation. When the time arrives, proceed to arrest the target(s) with a designated arrest team, specifying who will be involved and who will not.

Each undercover mission required thorough planning, often taking weeks to tackle the previously mentioned questions. Launching an undercover operation without sufficient preparation would be sheer recklessness.

Before commencing a specific case, I readied myself for undercover work by investigating the suspects and spending time with them. I aimed to understand who I would encounter and their relationships to avoid any unforeseen surprises from someone who might recognize me. The last thing I wanted was to be in a situation with a criminal when one of his acquaintances, someone I had previously arrested, unexpectedly appeared. Not only would this compromise my cover, but it could also pose a serious danger to my safety.

While conducting undercover work, I learned that it's essential to remain true to yourself to avoid remembering too many lies, as there are no second takes. You do not want the bad guy to catch you in a lie because this can quickly lead to consequences and even cause harm. Create a story and stick to it; do not change anything.

When operating undercover, the most challenging aspect was keeping my undercover backstory and my partner's straight. Whether undercover or not, I often referred to my partners by their undercover names. This habit became more instinctive around others, although errors did occur.

During an undercover meeting with a suspect, I recall an instance when my partner accidentally used my real name. We somehow navigated that moment, but the culprits didn't catch on. There was even a time when I called my partner by his real name, and no one noticed.

I know firsthand that living a "double life" wasn't easy and often took its toll on me. It was tough on Linda and Jacob, even though they never knew what I was doing at work. I kept them out of everything because there was no need for them to know. Sometimes, it was challenging to maintain perspective between my work in Baton Rouge and my life in Amite. I remember that when the workplace called, you were there. Nonetheless, I was proud to have had the opportunity to work with some great officers and to be part of putting some bad guys behind bars.

Countless nights found me in bars and even more dangerous places, working undercover to buy narcotics and weapons while posing as someone else. Afterward, I would return home and struggle to reconnect with my true self around Linda and Jacob. Many times, I would walk outside of the house and look up and down the street. Who was passing by? Do I know the vehicle? I had to make sure no one followed me home or learned where I lived. It wasn't me I was worried about; I couldn't let anything happen to Linda or Jacob. Paranoid? Maybe a little bit, but there were times when I saw a vehicle pass by my house and didn't know it. I jumped in my vehicle and followed it to see where it went. Yeah, I was a little paranoid, but I knew what specific outcomes could be, and I wasn't going to let that happen.

After work, I varied my routes home and paused now and then to see if anyone was following me, as the last thing I wanted was a criminal on my tail. It's crucial to mention that certain primary drug dealers maintained their own "police force" for protection. This involved keeping an eye on potential buyers to collect information via surveillance. Some criminals operated with a level of sophistication, using their financial resources to avoid detection. Remember, they have plenty of money to afford the equipment and resources needed to protect their operations.

Take a moment to reflect on our perceptions of drug dealers; various portrayals from movies and television might come to mind. Yet, the truth is much more intricate. Recognize that a drug dealer can range from a street-level dealer to a prominent figure within an organized crime group. They can emerge from all societal strata; through conversations with many, I've discovered that each has a distinct narrative and rationale behind their choices.

For many, the chance to quickly earn money and gain influence serves as a powerful motivator. The potential for swift and significant financial rewards can relieve economic stress, yet the attraction of quick cash is hard to resist. Some drug dealers can make in a single day what they would usually earn in a month with a traditional job. This is undeniably a tempting offer, particularly for those who feel confined by poverty and view their life opportunities as limited.

However, it's not merely about financial gain; being a dealer also confers power. In certain areas, becoming a drug dealer can quickly enhance one's status, transforming them from an everyday community member into an influential figure, evoking both respect and fear. The leader of an operation operates by instilling fear in those around them, which keeps everyone in line. So, what motivates individuals to enter the drug trade? This decision is not taken lightly, and the reasons vary just as much as the individuals who pursue this route.

Often, I felt that my true life was on the streets of Baton Rouge, amongst the drug dealers and thieves, while my undercover existence was in Amite with Linda and Jacob. Many times, it became a heavy burden for me, to the point of making me ill.

After a long night or several days away from home, knowing what I had to do and the drugs I bought for work made it extremely hard for me to return home and face Linda and Jacob. Sometimes, I felt so disgusted at home and worried about what Linda would think of me if she knew what I was doing. I kept trying to convince myself that I was fighting crime, putting bad guys in jail, and all that good stuff. I was doing everything I could to persuade myself that I was doing the right thing. Somehow, I managed to get through those times and rough feelings to move on, but it hardened my heart, mind, and even my soul.

On my days off at home, while playing with Jacob, I often thought about how he would view me if he knew my job. Just hours before returning home, I found myself among drug dealers and some truly terrible individuals, pretending to fit in. I frequently wished I could look into Jacob's innocent eyes and express my regret, explaining that I wasn't the person I pretended to be. Spending time with him allowed me to forget about work, even if only for a brief moment.

In my undercover assignments, I teamed up with a top agent who met all my professional and personal requirements. Rather than going to the narcotics office, I operated an undercover vehicle, occasionally rotating it. I would use the same vehicle only when I had built a rapport with someone and was involved in continuous discussions.

I kept my distance from other police officers while I was out to avoid blowing my cover. Most officers were aware of which personnel were assigned undercover, so when they saw us, we were never approached. I regularly met with my top agent to provide information and submit reports or evidence (including drugs) that I had acquired. There were times when I purchased narcotics and wanted to submit them into evidence as quickly as possible. The top agent managed my reports and evidence to ensure the integrity of the case I was building.

Occasionally, I would meet with my supervisor to approve additional purchasing funds or submit receipts for previous expenses and cash payments. Although it was quite a hassle, it was necessary. Obtaining receipts from bars and clubs was challenging since I paid in cash instead of using credit cards.

Getting Attached

After years of covert operations, I realized that it made me somewhat rigid in my thinking.

Working undercover is incredibly stressful. Once you take on an undercover role, you become disconnected from everyone familiar, particularly your family. You must adopt behaviors and false identities that starkly contrast with your own beliefs and personality. This situation often attracts negative attention from the public and, at times, from colleagues. Frequently, this can lead to issues regarding mental and even physical health. Unsurprisingly, it complicates the process of readjusting socially with family and friends after the assignment is complete.

Undercover operations have significantly influenced law enforcement by enabling the infiltration of criminal organizations and revealing their activities. They provide insights into individuals that law enforcement typically struggles to expose. By employing undercover tactics, intelligence can be gathered, and concealed illegal actions can be unearthed.

Conducting undercover operations is burdened with risks and dangers. Numerous ethical dilemmas must be addressed, and the psychological well-being of the undercover agent needs careful monitoring. Each undercover case requires thorough planning and well-considered scenarios, with every participant needing to commit fully to their role. There can be no weak links in this chain.

Now, while working undercover, you meet a lot of people,

and not all are bad. In numerous cases I worked, I was introduced to a bad guy who sold me drugs whenever I requested. He also invited me to family functions, cookouts, and birthday parties. I would attend to keep my relationship with the bad guy, but while at these functions, I met family members who had no clue that their "knuckle-headed" relative was selling drugs to me and others. They were nice people and, over time, accepted me as a friend to the family and even invited me to their home on many occasions. I did my best to avoid as much interaction as possible because I knew what would be coming down the road. Also, some of these people were very wealthy, living in big homes and had great jobs.

I was once invited to a family wedding because I had allowed myself to become too close to the family members. I didn't want to, but I attended so that my relationship with the family wouldn't be hindered.

After eight months of working with this individual and generating numerous cases by introducing him to others, along with my ability to bring in other agents, we decided to shut down the operation and make all the arrests. We also executed search warrants on several homes where we purchased narcotics.

I was there when we apprehended my suspect, and he

laughed, believing I was pretending to be a cop with a fake badge. He asked questions like, "Where did you get the badge?" and "Who were all my friends?" When it came time to face the truth, his expression and the words he shared with me privately have stayed with me ever since. Even now, I remember his face and the look of betrayal. I allowed him to get too close, but I did what was necessary. He cried upon learning the truth, and that was the last time I saw him as he left that courtroom.

I wasn't needed at the search warrants conducted at their residences. Nonetheless, the truth is that this individual posed a significant issue. He not only distributed large quantities of drugs but also knew about extensive narcotics operations and links to dangerous individuals. These individuals contributed to the distribution of harmful substances within the community.

This man served three years in prison, and several others did the same.

I never spoke with the family members after that. However, about six months later, the mother called me and wanted to meet with me to discuss the situation. I arranged for her to come into the 3rd District precinct, where we met and talked for about an hour.

She was confused about her son and what he was involved in, and she had no clue about the drug sales. The indication I got from her was that she was hurt, but not by me; it was her son. I explained to her about the help her son could receive while in prison, and when he comes out, he should be able to start a new life or have a new beginning.

Following our meeting, I reached out occasionally to ensure she was okay. She mentioned that many family members were upset with me and held me responsible for the situation. However, she recognized that it was her son's fault, not mine. She also remarked that every dark cloud has a silver lining. After a few check-ins, I eventually lost touch with her and never spoke to her again.

This case provided me with invaluable insights. I've realized how crucial it is to reassess and carefully evaluate each decision. Ultimately, our goal is to apprehend drug dealers and weapons smugglers, removing them from the streets. It took a while to overcome situations like these, but I couldn't deny that my heart and conscience grew somewhat hardened.

However, at the time, returning to Linda and Jacob after cases kept me grounded in reality. With them, I convinced myself that this is me, this is who I am, a husband and a father.

Chapter 7

Take a Step Back

At times, it's essential to step back and take a break to let things settle. Stepping away from your previous activities gives rivals and others a chance to momentarily forget about you. When you feel rejuvenated, you'll be ready to re-enter the scene and pick up where you left off. Briefly disconnecting from the artificial world and reconnecting with reality can help clear your thoughts and strengthen your connection to yourself.

Motorcycle Division

After years in narcotics, I recognized the need for a break from drugs and the nightlife. I sought opportunities to learn or engage in activities that could transform my life.

I've held various positions in the police force, but I had never had the chance to ride motorcycles for the department. Riding for the Baton Rouge Police Department (BRPD) had always been a dream of mine. I remember admiring motorcyclists as they cruised around the city—it seemed exhilarating, which motivated me to give it a try.

I inquired with several supervisors and spoke with multiple motorcycle officers to gain their insights into the position. I completed the necessary paperwork and officially submitted my request to transfer to the Traffic Division, Motorcycle Unit. I believed this decision would significantly reduce my stress and allow me to pursue something other than buying drugs.

Shortly after reflecting on the opportunity, a vacancy arose in the Motorcycle Unit. I submitted my transfer request to the Captain of the Traffic Division. After some time without a response, I assumed they had chosen another candidate for the role.

In late July 1985, I was surprised by a request to attend an interview at the Traffic Division and to take a motorcycle driving test. I participated in the interview and completed the motorcycle test. I also took a written examination at the office, passed all the tests, and a supervisor informed me that I would be notified if selected.

On August 1, 1985, I was informed of my selection for the position, which led to my transfer to the Motorcycle Division. I soon realized how much I enjoyed riding motorcycles and felt honored to represent the department on two wheels. This change brought a refreshing pace to my life; while I no longer dealt with the stress of drug transactions, I now faced the stress and challenge of overseeing city traffic.

Officers assigned to motorcycles were known as motor

officers or "motor men." Motorcycles were more maneuverable on crowded streets compared to larger, traditional police vehicles. They allowed us to quickly reach automobile accident scenes and navigate routes inaccessible to other vehicles, including narrow streets and footpaths.

Motorcycles were also utilized for police escorts during parades, funeral processions, motorcades, and other special events. We primarily used motorcycles for enforcing traffic laws and as patrol vehicles.

During my shift, I set up at various locations around the city to write traffic tickets or respond to vehicle accidents. I issued between 20 and 50 tickets a day for traffic violators. The ticket books contained 25 tickets, and our supervisors required us to issue at least one book per shift, which wasn't a problem for me, as people often ran stop signs and red lights throughout the city.

Until I officially began riding motorcycles, I never realized how many reckless drivers were on city roads. Everyone seemed to be in a hurry to reach their destinations, and few noticed motorcycles on the street.

In addition to my daily work, I took on extra assignments, such as escorting funerals and working at high school and LSU football games. For these additional duties, I received separate pay for each funeral I escorted. Before my shift, I was assigned to escort between two and four funerals. It was easier to do this on my day off, and I aimed to work as much as possible. If I recall correctly, I earned $35 per escort, whether it was a short one lasting an hour or a long one lasting several hours.

During the LSU and high school football seasons, I oversaw traffic and facilitated the safe flow of individuals in and out of parking lots. After the games concluded and the congestion subsided, my responsibilities were fulfilled, allowing me to head home.

Working at LSU football games was unique because I assisted with parking thousands of vehicles. To do this, I arrived several hours before the game started to attend a strategy meeting and discuss where each motorcycle officer would be stationed for traffic control.

I interacted with fans eager to park and enter the stadium quickly, as they didn't want to miss any of the action. This eagerness, however, often led to impatient drivers, which made the roads extremely hazardous.

While working at an LSU football game, I was riding my motorcycle on Acadian Drive, heading toward the LSU stadium. I was in the left lane, approaching an intersection to block traffic. Suddenly, a woman driving a van in the right lane next to me made an illegal left turn directly in front of me. We were both heading in the same direction toward the stadium when she turned left from her right lane, crossing into mine. I crashed my motorcycle into the driver's side of her van. Fortunately, she wasn't injured, but I hurt my left knee and needed medical treatment. The entire front of my bike was damaged and had to be towed; however, it was eventually repaired, and I was back on the road again.

I quickly discovered that motorcycle officers enjoyed playing tricks on one another for laughs. One night, I was assigned to work with other officers at a high school football game. It was cold, and I wasn't looking forward to the ride back home to Amite. When the game ended, I hurried to my motorcycle and jumped on it, eager to go home. I pressed the starter button, and at that moment, I felt the shock of my life in my crotch. Besides startling me, the pain was unbearable. I jumped off, unsure of what had happened, while the other police motorcycles took off, leaving me behind. My bike fell to the ground when I leapt off.

Before I could figure out what happened, I needed to get the bike upright and determine the cause. I knew something had shocked me, and it hurt, but what? After my investigation, I discovered that several officers had taken a thin metal wire, tied it around the spark plug head, ran it across the seat, and secured it to a part of the metal frame that would ground it. By doing this, when I pushed the starter switch, I received a shock in my crotch.

After getting my motorcycle upright with the help of a few people, I disconnected the wire, making it safe to start and head home. Following that incident, I learned a lot about the tricks that could be played while riding motorcycles. Every time I got on my motorcycle, I ran my hand across the seat to check for that wire. It was a joke meant to be fun, but it still hurt. Later, I got to play the same trick on someone else, and it was funny!

I quickly discovered another skill that riding motorcycles required. Before continuing, I want to emphasize that motorcycle officers are brave and unafraid to ride. When I joined their ranks, I had to learn all the tricks that could be played on me, and it's crucial to check a few things before hopping on your motorcycle. First, look for any wires on your seat, then verify the gas switch on the carburetor. This switch regulates the gas flow to and from the carburetor.

Unbelievably, some pranksters would turn your gas switch to the off position without you knowing. You may wonder why they would do that, so let me explain: turning the switch off leaves only a small amount of gas in the carburetor bowl, allowing you to drive approximately 50 feet before the engine shuts off. I often saw officers jump on their motorcycles, leave the traffic office, and, as soon as they merged onto Florida Boulevard, their motorcycles would shut off, causing them to fall over in the middle of the street.

Some of the tricks played were dangerous, but they aimed to teach you to inspect your motorcycle each time before riding. Anyone could perform these tricks, sometimes for malicious reasons, turning them into a lesson in hard knocks; ultimately, however, they kept you safe.

It's crucial to acknowledge numerous instances where officers, while attending to traffic accidents or other police matters, had their motorcycles' gas shut off by passersby unbeknownst to them. This led to several accidents.

Back to Uniform Patrol

Having served as a burglary detective, undercover narcotics officer, general detective, and motorcycle officer, I decided to seek a new direction. Although I considered returning to uniform patrol, after reflecting on it for some time, I ultimately convinced myself to move forward with that choice.

On January 1, 1986, I left the Traffic Division, gave up my motorcycle, and joined the Uniform Patrol Division on

Coursey Boulevard, known as the 3rd District. I started my tenure in uniform patrol at Winborn Station, but my time there was short before I was transferred to SPOT. Returning to uniform patrol provided me with the experience I had missed at Winborn.

In the Uniform Patrol Division, I patrolled an area within my assigned district, responded to various calls, conducted preliminary investigations into crimes, and enforced both criminal and traffic laws.

During my years with BRPD, I attended numerous training seminars, schools, and classes, including those offered by the Scientific Crime Investigators Institute, Interview and Interrogation Schools, firearms classes, and various law enforcement training programs. I participated in Field Training Officer School, Undercover Narcotics Training, Intoxilyzer School, and Tactical Police Driving School, among others.

Training was vital for effective policing, and I eagerly embraced every opportunity to participate in classes. Police training equipped me to manage potential challenges more adeptly and laid the groundwork for a successful law enforcement career.

Chapter 8

Small Town Police vs. Large City Police

Officers in larger cities gain "beat" experience more rapidly than those in smaller communities. Conversely, patrol officers in smaller towns often develop investigative skills at a faster pace.

There is no doubt that small-town police departments encounter challenges similar to those in larger cities, but a significant difference exists: they typically have considerably fewer resources and personnel. This disparity can hinder policing in these communities, especially when only one or two officers are available at a time. Consequently, smaller departments must focus on developing more efficient strategies rather than simply working harder.

Small-town police departments differ from the predominant big-city model, embodying a unique style of policing in the United States. Crucially, the insights gained from small-town policing can apply to urban settings.

As American society becomes more diverse, major city police departments should strive to replicate the successes of small-town police forces by adopting their strategies and practices. For instance, cities often divided into ethnic neighborhoods, each with its own cultural identity, could approach each neighborhood as a distinct community with its own police force.

The centralized structure standard in urban police departments should be reevaluated, allowing local precinct leaders the flexibility to adapt their approaches based on the unique needs of their communities. This decentralization would require a dependable unit of officers who reside in the neighborhoods they patrol.

Similar to small towns, neighborhoods in large cities often have precinct police stations that operate largely independently of the central headquarters, which aims to standardize policing across the city. Like their small-town counterparts, these trusted officers are committed to improving the quality of life for residents. They maintain open communication lines to ensure information flows effectively, which is vital for crime prevention and resolution.

In larger departments, specialized units handle specific job types. In contrast, officers in small-town policing encounter a variety of situations and often respond first to incidents, such as traffic accidents or homicides. A small-town officer may assume multiple roles, such as search and rescue operator, coroner, family therapist, or sex crimes investigator.

Officers in rural areas often have ongoing personal interactions with community members, and community policing is typically taken for granted. Knowing individuals in the community provides officers with insight into what to expect and how to engage. A peace officer who is familiar with a family and understands the habits of an offender benefits from informal social control.

When I initially shared my aspiration to become a police officer with Linda, she expressed concerns about the dangerous situations I might encounter and worried for my safety. I respected her apprehensions, yet I recognized that while a career in law enforcement can be fulfilling and rewarding, it also entails the risk of potentially sacrificing my life. I considered these factors before deciding to pursue this profession.

Many others cautioned me about the risks associated with this field, but I remained resolute in my commitment to face the job's challenges. Perhaps I was somewhat naïve, failing to fully grasp those dangers when I first embarked on this journey.

I acknowledged the risks, but because I had not yet personally experienced them, I could manage those possibilities more easily.

My ambition to pursue a career in law enforcement stemmed from multiple influences. Reflecting on my colleagues' experiences, I've come to understand that this career extends beyond wearing a badge. It involves making a meaningful difference in my community while upholding the principles of integrity and ethical law enforcement.

I aimed to be an officer who would overcome challenges and remain faithful to my values and beliefs, no matter what I faced or witnessed on the job. I wanted to inspire others to value and respect the profession of law enforcement.

Another aspect of law enforcement is the camaraderie that develops among fellow officers. When officers in a police department work closely together, everyone, including supervisors, takes notice. Some officers are easier to work with than others due to personality and individual interests. Over time, you may find it easier to build friendships with specific individuals.

Chapter 9

Dealing with Stress

Stress is an inescapable aspect of everyday life. While it can sometimes act as a motivator, aiding concentration, certain stressors can be harmful. For example, stress may drive you to complete a work project promptly, but the frustration of being stuck in traffic offers no benefits. We cannot eliminate all sources of stress, but learning to manage it can prevent harmful effects. Unmanaged stress can lead to negative responses, such as anger, and prolonged exposure can adversely affect our health in numerous ways.

Identifying when something causes stress and impacts us is an essential first step. A proven method to alleviate stress is practicing deep breathing exercises. Focusing on your breath rather than the stressor promotes relaxation.

Physical exercise offers another way to unwind. When confronted with stress, consider stepping outside for a brief walk and focusing on your surroundings instead of the stressor. This will promote relaxation and enhance mental clarity.

Learning to relax involves finding ways to redirect your thoughts and focus. Feeling frustrated by a traffic jam? Try turning on the car radio and singing along to the music. This approach helps you unwind by focusing on something enjoyable.

It's essential to prepare yourself to handle stress, as it will always be present. Maintaining good nutrition, exercising regularly, staying hydrated, and ensuring adequate rest are effective strategies to protect against stress's negative effects. Recognize when stress impacts you and integrate relaxation into your routine for beneficial results.

As a police officer, I understood the importance of maintaining public safety and responding to calls promptly. Over time, I gained experience in dealing with potentially dangerous suspects and crime victims, requiring me to remain calm and professional under pressure.

I also worked closely with community members to build relationships and ensure everyone felt safe in their neighborhood. Additionally, I acquired extensive knowledge of law enforcement procedures and protocols, enabling me to make quick decisions when necessary.

Building trust and fostering positive relationships with communities is one of the greatest challenges facing law enforcement today. The rise of social media and a stream of negative news stories contribute to growing distrust of police among many individuals. This negative perception creates hesitancy to engage with law enforcement, complicating efforts to solve crimes and ensure public safety.

Chapter 10

Ethics and Integrity

In my view, integrity is the most important quality for a police officer. A strong moral compass and steadfast dedication to the law are essential in all situations, especially challenging or dangerous ones, as they ensure justice and public safety. Additionally, respect for the law, excellent communication skills, empathy, physical fitness, and sound decision-making are vital characteristics of an effective police officer.

Integrity is defined by honesty and a strong commitment to moral and ethical principles in one's actions. Upholding integrity is linked to higher self-esteem and professional success. It embodies self-reflection, accountability, honesty, and ethical decision-making.

Integrity means doing what is right, even when unnoticed, serving as a moral compass that guides one's actions in life.

For success, a police officer must embody integrity and honesty, remain calm and collected in challenging situations, and possess effective communication skills. Taking initiative and staying physically fit are essential.

Officers should also demonstrate strong problem-solving

abilities and a thorough knowledge of the law and the community they serve. A successful police officer must have a genuine passion for their role and a dedication to protecting and serving others.

Research indicates a strong connection between integrity and self-esteem, suggesting that individuals with integrity exhibit higher levels of self-esteem. By fostering a sense of purpose, integrity contributes positively to self-esteem and overall well-being.

Integrity is vital in personal relationships and has a profound effect in the workplace. From my observations, leaders who demonstrate integrity cultivate a positive work environment characterized by trust, job satisfaction, and strong employee engagement.

By adhering to moral and ethical principles, these leaders promote a culture that emphasizes employee well-being, resulting in enhanced productivity and organizational success. This supportive atmosphere is one that everyone appreciates.

I believe an individual can work in law enforcement while upholding strong moral character, provided personal agendas do not interfere.

I always believed in upholding the law and aspired to be a

law enforcement officer who could serve as a role model. I recall my first job with the Amite Police Department (APD), but I don't remember planning to change careers.

I served my community in Amite by consistently maintaining public safety. I felt that the people of Amite respected me and my fellow officers because I prioritized setting a good example of honest police work.

Capable officers can make a positive impact by upholding a significant purpose. When a police department operates efficiently, the crime rate can decrease, fostering a greater sense of safety among community members. Moreover, justice is served when investigations are conducted meticulously, evidence is handled with diligence and respect, and perpetrators are held accountable.

Effective communication is essential for resolving conflicts, even among colleagues. I understand that disagreements can arise, and I always strive to remain professional and neutral when handling them. My strategy involves engaging in calm conversations, actively listening to the other officer's perspective, and working together to find a resolution. Having managed difficult situations and disputes, I am confident in my ability to handle conflicts respectfully and effectively.

Conclusion

Joining the Baton Rouge Police Department (BRPD) was a pivotal decision that presented both benefits and challenges. It allowed me to serve my community, forge meaningful connections, and experience the fulfillment of safeguarding others. However, the role also entailed significant stress, long hours, and personal sacrifices.

As I prepared to leave the BRPD, memories of my conversations with APD Officer Jeff Alston resurfaced. I recalled his insights on what to expect at the BRPD academy, the realities of working patrol, and the benefits of patrolling with my driver's window open. Jeff's guidance was invaluable; his advice greatly supported me throughout my nine-plus years at the BRPD. I attribute my professional development within the BRPD and the vital training for federal employment to Jeff.

As a police officer, I adapted to daily changes. I attended meetings, wrote reports, patrolled the city, and responded to various emergency calls. My success was rooted in key traits, including attention to detail, empathy, and a strong sense of justice.

Over time, I encountered several career opportunities, including roles as a patrol officer, detective, narcotics agent, and motorcycle officer, among others.

The public had high expectations of me, particularly regarding compassion. I recall engaging with many individuals during their difficult times.

As a police officer, part of my role was to comfort a distressed victim, interview a witness to a tragic event, and treat a suspect with dignity and respect. These elements are essential aspects of the profession.

Demonstrating compassion while assisting others and prioritizing their needs above my own allowed me to handle situations effectively. Empathy and compassion are essential for a successful career.

Initially, compassion and empathy were not natural for me. Despite my efforts to cultivate these traits, I found them challenging. However, I recognized they existed within me.

Over time, I discovered that helping others through emotional hardships nurtured the compassion I needed to be an effective officer.

I was truly a people person, engaging with a diverse array of individuals, including victims, witnesses, criminals, and community members. My strong interpersonal skills were vital for interacting with the public during stressful and tense situations.

Programs at the police academy helped me develop interpersonal skills. However, a personality trait will enhance your capabilities only if you actively cultivate it.

My son, Jacob, makes friends effortlessly and engages in conversation with anyone, regardless of the situation. He possesses the crucial interpersonal skills needed for success. His ability to converse with anyone is an excellent skill, as it can lead to new friendships or uncover career and business opportunities. Humans are social beings by nature, but conversation does not come naturally to everyone.

I was also required to have strong communication skills, as I needed to converse effectively with others. It was crucial to listen and express thoughts clearly in high-stress situations and to utilize both verbal and nonverbal communication. I successfully communicated with suspects, witnesses, and fellow law enforcement personnel.

Understanding others' reactions and knowing how to persuade and negotiate were crucial during challenging situations.

When I began my career, I realized I could stay composed in a crisis and effectively address others' panic. Over time, I learned to handle the pressures of being a police officer.

I found joy in serving because I was required to protect and serve in ways that extended beyond my vision as a law enforcement officer.

I often found myself first on the scene during emergencies, which allowed me to influence others positively. Whether gathering facts to comfort crime victims or assisting stranded motorists, I made a difference and built connections with them. I recall numerous instances where I exceeded my duties by performing small acts of kindness to support those in need.

My decision to pursue a career in law enforcement was not frivolous. It was a tremendous honor to be entrusted with the safety and security of my community. Although I didn't know everything expected of me, I learned quickly and did my best to fulfill those responsibilities.

I chose law enforcement because I thought it would be thrilling. Although I aimed to assist others, it was the exciting aspects of the job, such as responding to hazardous situations and apprehending criminals, that attracted me most.

After my initial six months, my actions reflected not those of a young, naïve individual but those of a genuine police officer—one with the authority to restrict someone's freedom or, in extreme situations, their life.

I also came to understand that while the job had grown more daunting, it simultaneously became a greater honor, inspiring me to work harder to ensure I did things correctly.

I conducted extensive research on law enforcement and completed numerous courses in criminal justice. I have always been passionate about a career in this field, driven by my desire to impact my community positively. I believe there is no position more privileged than working in law enforcement.

As I mentioned earlier, Linda expressed concerns about me facing dangerous situations and worried about my safety. I understood that this career could involve risking my life, and I was aware of this when I chose this profession.

I aspired to be an officer capable of defying all odds while remaining true to my values and convictions, regardless of what I encountered on the job.

Federal Law Enforcement

After spending more than nine years with the BRPD, I began considering a career in federal law enforcement. I applied to the U.S. Border Patrol.

In May 1988, I started training at the U.S. Border Patrol Academy and was later stationed in Marfa, Texas. In Border

Patrol, I worked on the Southern border apprehending illegal migrants, drug smugglers, human traffickers, and suspected terrorists. I also worked in Immigration Inspections at airports and Ports of Entry, holding Special Agent and Supervisory Special Agent positions.

In my upcoming book, *U.S. Immigration Through My Eyes*, I will delve into the intricacies of working on the southern border and investigating immigration type cases.

I will explore the challenges related to alien smuggling, human trafficking, and the smuggling of drugs and weapons, all of which I encountered firsthand in Marfa.

www.ingramcontent.com/pod-product-compliance
Lightning Source LLC
Chambersburg PA
CBHW050735010526
44107CB00010B/865